Kundalini Awakening for Beginners

2 Books in 1: Expand Mind Power, Astral Travel, Chakra Meditation, Learn Psychic Abilities, Open Your Third Eye and More

Lisa Blake

© Copyright 2020 by Lisa Blake. All rights reserved.

The work contained herein has been produced with the intent to provide relevant knowledge and information on the topic described in the title for entertainment purposes only. While the author has gone to every extent to furnish up to date and true information, no claims can be made as to its accuracy or validity as the author has made no claims to be an expert on this topic. Notwithstanding, the reader is asked to do their own research and consult any subject matter experts they deem necessary to ensure the quality and accuracy of the material presented herein.

This statement is legally binding as deemed by the Committee of Publishers Association and the American Bar Association for the territory of the United States. Other jurisdictions may apply their own legal statutes. Any reproduction, transmission or copying of this material contained in this work without the express written consent of the copyright holder shall be deemed as a copyright violation as per the current legislation in force on the date of publishing and subsequent time thereafter. All additional works derived from this material may be claimed by the holder of this copyright.

The data, depictions, events, descriptions and all other information forthwith are considered to be true, fair and accurate unless the work is expressly described as a work of fiction. Regardless of the nature of this work, the Publisher is exempt from any responsibility of actions taken by the reader in conjunction with this work. The Publisher acknowledges that the reader acts of their own accord and releases the author and Publisher of any responsibility for the observance of tips, advice, counsel, strategies and techniques that may be offered in this volume.

TABLE OF CONTENTS

Open Your Third Eye

Ultimate Guide to Open Your Third Eye and Awaken Your Chakras to Enhance Psychic Abilities and Decalcify Pineal Gland

INTRODUCTION 2

Chapter 1 *The Third Eye* 4

    Location and Function of Your Third Eye 4

    Correspondences of the Third Eye 6

    Responsibilities of the Third Eye 7

Chapter 2 *Symptoms Of A Blocked Third Eye* 9

    Key Characteristics of the Third Eye Chakra 9

Chapter 3 *Benefits Of A Healthy Third Eye* 13

Chapter 4 *Methods For Opening Your Third Eye* 15

    Yoga for Opening the Third Eye 18

    Affirmations for Opening the Third Eye 18

    Color for Opening the Third Eye 20

Chapter 5 *The Third Eye Doorway To The Psychic World* 22

    Psychic Readings with Mediums 22

    Relaxation, Emptiness, and Meditation 24

    Psychic Sense with Automatic Writing 27

    Psychic Power with Extrasensory Perception (ESP) 30

    The Eight Limbs of Mind Yoga 31

Chapter 6 *Consciousness Of The Third Eye* 35

    The Third Eye States of Consciousness 35

Third Eye Etheric Vision 37

The Third Eye and Temporal Vision 39

Third Eye Spirituality and Mysticism 39

Third Eye Psychic Visions 41

The Tunnel of the Third Eye 43

Telepathic Awareness 44

Chapter 7 *Astral Beings And The Third Eye* **46**

Other Worlds 46

Traveling the Astral Planes 47

Out of Body Experiences 48

Dream Control 51

Chapter 8 *Spiritual Beings And The Third Eye* **54**

Earthbound Spirits 54

Knowing your Spirit Guide 55

Earth Angel 58

Divination 59

Precognition and Spirituality 61

Etheric Entities on the Physical Plane 62

Chapter 9 *Life After Life* **64**

Elevated Souls on Earth 64

Daydreams for Life 65

Dreaming and Symbolism 68

Awareness of the Aura 69

Seeing into the Afterlife 70

Reincarnation 71

Chapter 10 *Improved Life With An Open Third Eye* 73

Conclusion 77

Kundalini

Expand Mind Power, Gain Spiritual Awareness, Open Your Third Eye, Enhance Psychic Abilities and Discover Transcendence

INTRODUCTION **79**

Chapter 1 *What Is Mind Power?* **80**

    The Kundalini Take on Mind Power 80

    The Power of Your Thoughts 81

    Exercising Your Creative Power 82

    Reality at a Thought-Level 83

Chapter 2 *A Clear Overview Of Physical Mind Power* **85**

    Neuroplasticity and Neural Pathways 85

    Mental Stimulation for Improved Mind Power 86

    Physical Exercise and Dietary Considerations 87

    Maintaining a Healthy Bodily Function 88

    Caring for Your Emotional Wellbeing 89

Chapter 3 *A Mind-Expanding Diet* **91**

    The Tridoshas 91

    The Types of Food 92

    Eating for Your Doshas 93

Chapter 4 *Yoga And Mind Power* **103**

    The Snake in Your Spine 103

    White and Kundalini Yoga 103

Tuning in for Your Session 103

Kundalini Kriyas and Mantra 104

Chapter 5 *Relationships And Mind Power* 106

Creating Strong Relationships in Your Life 107

Using Relationships as a Point of Growth 108

How Relationships Affect Your Spiritual Energy 109

Chapter 6 *The Number One Mind Power Killer* 111

The Secret Killer of Mind Power... 111

How This Killer Affects Your Energy 111

How to Spot the Killer 112

What to Do About It 113

Protecting Yourself From It 114

Chapter 7 *The Mindset Aspects Of Mind Power* 116

How Mindset Controls Your Mind Power 116

The Mindset That Unlocks Your Potential 117

Awakening Your Kundalini Mindsets 118

Incorporating a New Mindset Into Your Life 118

Chapter 8 *Having A Growth Mindset* 120

Growth Mindset Vs. Fixed Mindset 120

Kundalini and Growth Mindset 121

Be Conscious About What You Feed Your Mind 121

Work on Your Desire 121

Have the Right Sources 122

Embrace a Drive to Learn 122

Stay Open and Flexible 122

Be Creative and Successful 123

Release Others' Influence Over You 123

Surround Yourself With Positivity 124

Speak of Present Success 124

Work Through Your Resistance 125

Chapter 9 *Deepening Your Sense Of Self* **126**

Dissolution of Your Self 126

Substantiation of Your New Self 127

Exploring Life With Your New Identity 128

Expanding Your Perception of Self 129

Chapter 10 *Using Your Mind As A Problem Solver* **131**

The Path of Ascended Problem Solving 131

Discovering a New Way for Everything 132

Becoming the Brightest Version of Yourself 133

Expanding Your Power to Others 134

Chapter 11 *Your Ego Needs Checking* **136**

Shedding the Programmed Ego 136

Preventing Your Ego From Holding You Back 137

Creating an Egoless Future 139

Chapter 12 *Happiness Is Your Choice, Make It* **140**

The Real Path to Happiness 140

How Happiness Improves Your Health 141

Consciously Choosing to Be Happy 141

Embracing a Lack of Happiness 142

Chapter 13 *How You Treat Them Is How You Treat You* **144**

Why Your Intrapersonal Relationship Matters 144

Expanding the Quality of Your Relationship to Self 145

Unconditional Love and Acceptance of Others 146

Empowering All From Your Expanded Awareness 147

Chapter 14 *Becoming Your Biggest Cheerleader* **149**

Feeling the Entirety of Your Presence 149

Celebrating Yourself on Every Level 149

Embracing Fearlessness In Your Life 150

Living as Your Authentic Self 150

Chapter 15 *Love Conquers All... Really* **152**

Love to Overcome Ego 152

Unconditional Love Is the Goal 153

The Eightfold Theory of Love 153

Chapter 16 *Set Goals And Accomplish Them, Often* **156**

The Achieve and Integrate Cycle 156

Setting Goals for Your Ascended Self 156

Reaching the Goals Energetically 157

Embodying Your Accomplishments 158

Chapter 17 *Create Healthy Habits* **159**

Physically Embodying Healthy Habits 160

Healthy Habits for Your Limitless Mind 160

Caring for Your Emotions With Healthy Habits 161

Nurturing Your Spirit With Healthy Habits 161

Chapter 18 *Open Yourself Up To Change* **163**

Embodying a Daily Kundalini Ritual 163

Opening Yourself Up to Change 163

Work With Change Intentionally 164

Being the Most Adaptable Version of Yourself 165

Chapter 19 *Exercise The Power Of Creativity* **166**

Creativity Is at the Root of Manifesting 166

Unlocking the Power of Your Creativity 167

Steps to Expand Your Creativity 168

Integrating Creativity Into Your Everyday Life 169

Conclusion **171**

Open Your Third Eye

Ultimate Guide to Open Your Third Eye and Awaken Your Chakras to Enhance Psychic Abilities and Decalcify Pineal Gland

Lisa Blake

INTRODUCTION

Congratulations on purchasing this book, and thank you for doing so.

The following chapters will discuss your Third Eye and its ability to bring power and enlightenment to your life. The mind's window to the universe and all of its power is located in the Third Eye. With an open Third Eye, you will have access to the knowledge of millions of souls that have gone on before, those who now inhabit the astral planes beyond your current field of vision. When the Third Eye is functioning, your brain will flood with light from the universe, and the details of your life will suddenly become clear to you. Your reality will change in ways you never dreamed were possible.

The power of your Third Eye drives all of your intuition and sixth sense. The people and events in your world will suddenly become clear. When you open your Third Eye to the possibilities around you, your inner vision will clear. You will know a new reality that is elevated far above anything you currently know. Your thoughts will be clear and valid. You will know your true inner feelings, and you will make them work for you.

The human mind and spirit are amazing things, but most people are so far removed from realizing their true potential. The real power lies in the Third Eye, and opening it will bring marvelous enlightenment. This enlightenment gives you the ability to know things you could not know before and see something you previously only dreamed about experiencing. This enlightenment will take you to Nirvana, where you will enjoy total peace and contentment. Until you reach this state, you are limited in what you can do and know, but when your Third Eye is functioning, you will achieve all of these things and more.

The abilities that all humans possess are still not understood by most. Conscious thought is one example of this. When a decision is made, and action follows, that action is tainted by the conscious and subconscious mind's knowledge. Every reaction you have to any life event is driven by all your previous life experiences' cumulative effects. Your subconscious will take over when you do not have the time to rationalize the situation. When you have the time to think logically, you can decide on a course of action based on reason and fact. Too often, the subconscious mind takes over and drives your actions.

When your Third Eye is open, your mind will no longer be at war with itself. It will no longer be forced to choose between the conscious facts and the subconscious reasons that drive its actions. When your mind vibrates with the positive energy that comes with an open Third Eye, you will achieve the best possible decisions based on knowledge without discounting your feelings. Your conscious and subconscious minds will merge into one.

The influx of positive energy from the universe will enlighten your mind and create a spiritual transformation that will enable you to achieve true self-realization. Your Third Eye will awaken your intuition and psychic powers that are now lying unused inside you. You will possess insight that goes far beyond any everyday rational thinking you are currently used to knowing. Once you are willing to accept this transformation, there will no longer be limits on anything you wish to achieve.

There are plenty of books on the market on this subject; thanks again for choosing this one! Every effort was made to ensure it is full of as much useful information as possible; please enjoy!

CHAPTER 1
The Third Eye

One of the seven internal chakras is the Third Eye Chakra. It is the esoteric and mystical concept of the invisible, all-knowing eye, usually depicted as centered in the middle of the human forehead. The Third Eye will enable you to have a level of perception that goes far beyond ordinary sight. Ancient philosophers taught that the Third Eye was the location of the seat of your soul.

Location and Function of Your Third Eye

All people have the Third Eye, and everyone can access the powers of their own Third Eye if they choose to. Some people will use it with more intensity and more regularly than other people will. If you feel a feeling in your gut, that little nagging feeling that something isn't quite right, then you are collecting perceptions of the situation from your Third eye. These feelings are quite valid even if you cannot locate the source of information to justify your opinions with facts. Think of your Third Eye as a sense organ with unique powers that can be sharpened and improved with work. Your Third Eye will also help you read the signals from your environment and access your intuition to know the path you need to follow. It will also allow you to tune into the vibrations that come from other people. Strengthening your Third Eye use will help you connect with those whose energies match yours, and it will enhance your perceptions of life.

The Third Eye is the sixth internal chakra. It is referred to as the inner eye, the brow chakra, or the Third Eye Chakra. In Sanskrit, the word for the Third Eye is Ajna. This chakra determines how you evaluate your attitudes and beliefs as it correlates to your psychological skills and mental abilities. Located midway between your eyes, this gland is connected physically to your pineal gland, pituitary gland, and your brain. The energy of your psyche resonates through your Third Eye. This area is also where you will experience your unconscious and conscious psychological tendencies. In Eastern philosophies, the Third Eye is the spiritual center of your brain that works with the rational part of your mind to deepen your insight.

When your Third Eye opens, you will be challenged to discriminate between your thoughts motivated by illusion, fear, and strength. You will need to learn how to develop your impersonal mind and remove yourself from mental and physical illusions that cloud your perception of reality. You will have the ability to know your soul from deep within honestly and to overcome your fears, worries, and thoughts. Your Third Eye carries the personal combination of your unique experiences and concerns and facts that are continuously active within your mental body.

The basis of the Third Eye Chakra is truth. It wants to get to the heart of what is proper to decipher those thoughts from what you believe is right. Many of the facts that people hold are nothing more than the remnants of a negative memory from the past. Someone who has been told that they are ugly or fat will perceive themselves as ugly or fat, whether real or not. This belief is burned into their brain from mental conditioning. Opening the Third Eye will help you to rid yourself of such preconceived notions as this.

As the foundation of wisdom, the Third Eye wants to break down stereotypes and help you see past any preconceived notions you have developed. You will also gain detachment from societal realities and see beyond the illusions that the world at large will feed you. You will learn the ability to think freely when your freedom is able to go beyond the realms of the realistic. Nothing is holding you back besides the power that your mind holds over you. If you can regain control of your mind and your thoughts, you will rise above any limitations you have set for yourself.

A healthy and balanced Third Eye Chakra will make you realize that no one social group or individual can determine the path you will walk in life. The change will happen, and a larger karmic entity's dynamic will drive that change. This change will ignite a chain of events that will move you along the path towards your life's next stage. You might now think that other people's opinions have the power to manipulate you into doing things you aren't prepared or ready to do. But that idea is just an illusion that will hold you captive in a situation that you don't want to be in simply because you are not ready to make a change. You will rely on the opinions of others to tell you how to live your life.

It is essential for you to live your life on earth to your fullest and then to leave quietly when your Third Eye is open. Death is no longer something to fear. Rather, it is the doorway leading you to the continuing lesson of your existence. People are perfect when born, and they can leave this world as perfect beings. You create karmic manifestations in your life that cause you to feel pain or suffer from the disease. Your conscious mind can detach from affliction and evolve into the ability not to endure pain. Then the spirit can release from the body at the end of its time. This choice is available to anyone who wants it.

Correspondences of the Third Eye

Correspondences are items that go along with other items to create an effect that is either beneficial or harmful. Each of the chakras has certain things that correspond with them to help them be healthy and functional. These items come from many different areas. The medicinal benefits of various herbs have been recorded for centuries. Herbs provide powerful ingredients that, if used properly, can help heal your body. Your body's natural healing process will utilize the ingredients provided by nature with fresh herbs for its benefit. The fresh bark, leaves, and roots of herbs are best used in their natural form. Herbs are also used in dried form or used as tablets, tinctures, capsules, creams, lotions, essential oils, powders, and salves. The vibrational frequency of herbs is in tune with that of our bodies. The Third Eye's favorite herbs are lavender, juniper berry, chamomile, thyme, frankincense, tea tree, and eucalyptus.

Aromatherapy involves using naturally distilled essences made from flowers and herbs to improve the health of your body, spirit, mind, and emotions. Plant essences become essential oils, and they can restore harmony and balance to your body and improve your life. Essential oils made of fruit, herbs, and flower essences are concocted to center your body and mind and enhance your life. They work as preventative measures and are an effective cure for many illnesses. Scents can induce tremendous power as they influence your moods. The most direct path to your emotions is your sense of smell. This influence is the principle behind the ancient art of aromatherapy. The same herbs that you will use for herbal Third Eye therapy are used for aromatherapy.

Colors are also used as correspondences. You can wear clothing or wrap yourself in blankets and shawls of the color that corresponds to a particular chakra. You can imagine that you are bathed in a light of that color associated with your chakra during meditation. The Third Eye prefers the color indigo, a deep midnight blue that is a combination of violet and deep blue, and carries both colors' attributes. One power of the color indigo is service to humanity and empathy for all beings. Indigo is powerful and dignified, and it conveys deep integrity and sincerity. The color meaning of indigo reflects excellent devotion, wisdom, and justice, along with fairness and impartiality. It will defend people's rights to the end. Indigo stimulates the right side of your brain to enhance creative activity and assist with spatial skills. It is a dramatic hue.

As the sixth internal chakra, your Third Eye governs your sixth sense. When it is blocked, you may feel disoriented, which will cause you a lot of psychic and psychological stress. You will feel lost and confused in an endless stream of information and nonsensical vision. You might also start to indulge in too much fantasy and lose touch with reality. You can use healing crystals to unblock and heal this chakra. The best crystals for this purpose are amethyst, sodalite, unakite, clear quartz, Moldavite, clear quartz crystal, iolite, sapphire, and lapis lazuli.

Responsibilities of the Third Eye

The Third Eye controls different areas in your body, and the effect will show when the chakra itself is injured or blocked. The Third Eye Chakra correlates to your psychological skills, mental abilities, and how you evaluate attitudes and beliefs. Located between your eyes, this mind chakra is physically connected to your pineal gland, as well as your pituitary gland and your brain. It controls your psychological tendencies as well as holding the energy of your psyche.

People are often afraid to look within and see the flaws and faults they carry. Acknowledging your inner truth can be scary, and your reasoning might be faulty. You fear being criticized because of your inner darkness, what goes with it, and other people's opinions. Balancing this sixth chakra gives you spiritual awareness of knowing there is a time that is appropriate for all things in life. It gives you the ability to let go of old patterns of thought and embrace fresh new ones. Continuing to fear the unknown will deprive you of living life to the fullest. The health of your mind and body are directly affected by your thoughts and attitudes. Depression directly affects your immune system. Your body is not able to heal because it is listening to the negativity in your mind. Your healing process is hampered by negative emotions like anger, jealousy, bitterness, and resentment. Recovery needs the unity of your heart, mind, and body. An unhealthy Third Eye chakra brings on recurring depression, nightmares, headaches, sleep problems, and spiritual arrogance.

A structure the size of a green pea, your pineal gland is seated in the middle of your brain. Once a tool that was revered by seers and mystics, it's now mostly dormant. Whatever divine purpose it once had was lost with the passage of generations. The pineal gland helps to connect all the powers of the universe. Every culture throughout the world touts the significance of the pineal gland. When you develop the powers of your Third Eye and open the doorway to all things psychic, you will enjoy the powers of astral travel, controlled dreams, clairvoyance, and telepathy. You will realize your ability to communicate with the divine. When you learn to utilize the benefits of the pineal gland, the illusion of separation dissolves. Because the gland is inside your brain, but outside your mind, a paradox is formed, creating a loophole to escape the contradiction of your reality.

This chakra holds the ability to connect you to the universe and fill you with a power much more intense and mystical than anything you can know with your physical senses. With the opening of your Third Eye and the pineal gland it corresponds to, you will be able to achieve elevated powers that include psychic vision, and you will connect intimately with the Divine.

CHAPTER 2
Symptoms Of A Blocked Third Eye

Located in between your brows, the Third Eye chakra is responsible for how you perceive the world. The energy of your Third Eye chakra starts in-between your brows, just above the bridge of your nose. This chakra is responsible for linking your mind and the outer world, embodying your ability to see both the inner and outer worlds. You will experience clear thought and self-reflection.

Your Third Eye chakra is driven by reflection, knowledge, and intuition. It symbolizes your connection to insight and deep wisdom, allowing you access to the inner guidance that comes from deep within your being. This connection enables you to cut through illusion and access more profound truths. Your Third Eye gives you the gift of thoughtful living. It is the center of your intuition and wisdom. The energy of your Third Eye chakra starts in-between your brows, just above the bridge of your nose. This chakra is responsible for linking your mind and the outer world, embodying your ability to see both the inner and outer worlds. You will experience clear thought and self-reflection.

Your Third Eye chakra is driven by reflection, knowledge, and intuition. It symbolizes your connection to insight and deep wisdom, allowing you access to the inner guidance that comes from deep within your being. This connection enables you to cut through illusion and access more profound truths. Your Third Eye gives you the gift of thoughtful living in the present moment. Your intuition and wisdom gather in your Third Eye chakra, allowing you to open your mind to deeper understandings and expand your awareness. When this chakra is balanced, you possess the ability to reflect on your inner self and see the world and understand it.

Key Characteristics of the Third Eye Chakra
Logic & Creativity — you will possess the ability to integrate your imagination, creativity, and logical thinking.

Vision — this is the link between your conscious mind and the physical world. It enables you to internalize visions from the outer world and reflect on them within.

Self-Reflection — you will receive the ability to examine your motives and reflect on your actions without bias.

Wisdom — this center of wisdom and knowledge wills your mind to deeper understandings.

Intuition — your new abilities are instrumental in perceiving the subtle qualities of a new reality. You will open your mind to intuitive sensibility and inner perception.

Your chakra system distributes the flow of prana or energy throughout your subtle body. Stress, emotional upset, illness, or conflict can cause blockages or imbalance in your subtle body. The seven internal chakras are interconnected. A blockage or imbalance in one will affect the others, and an energy disruption like this can cause you to suffer in your mind, body, and spirit. A blocked Third Eye causes emotional and physical stress. Suppose you are developing a deeper understanding of your world and expanding your intuition. In that case, it is essential that you open and balance your Third Eye chakra.

Clear and intelligent perception comes from an open Third Eye. In between your eyebrows at the center of your forehead, the Third Eye holds the bridge between your emotional and mental perceptions of the world. Dynamic balance in the Third Eye gives you the ability to trust your intuition, see-through deception, and quickly cultivate self-reflection. When linked to extrasensory perception, this includes visually perceiving auras or spirit guides. A chakra can be blocked or suffer from over-activation of the energy within the chakras. A backup will create an aversion to allowing life to circulate through this chakra, whether that blockage is from stagnation or fear.

When this sixth chakra is blocked, telltale emotions that might flood your system include disregard for intuition or emotional intelligence, gullibility, having a closed mind, and becoming stuck in the rational thought process. Other emotions that may circulate include feeling unable to work well with emotions, mentally exhausted, quickly following propaganda, weak imagination, and a profoundly subconscious fear of the truth.

The overactive chakra is a gathering of energy within one energy center. This causes the entire chakra system to become imbalanced. This will display as a strong emotional attraction to specific Third Eye chakra characteristics. Drifting between reality and the imagination, suffering nightmares, and hallucinations, or living in a fantasy world are all emotional symptoms of an overactive Third Eye chakra. These include self-criticism, struggling to stay committed to prior commitments, trying to force a process, or paranoia.

There are definite symptoms that will tell you that your Third Eye is not healthy and needs more attention. Becoming obsessed with spiritual matters is another symptom. You might use spiritual teachings to suppress or avoid painful emotions or unresolved issues as an act of spiritual bypassing. You are not merely a physical body. You might feel lost with no sense of purpose or path in life. This can lead you to follow an undesirable idea or group that will give you a sense of meaningful purpose in your life.

Your overactive imagination might lead you down the wrong path. You spend too much time worrying and regretting it. You worry about your future and regret the things you did in the past. You imagine everything that might go wrong and spend too much time worrying about the imaginary negative things other people are saying about you. You might feel life is too frightening to consider if you do not take appropriate action immediately to fix your broken life. You become stuck in analyzing everything while you try to figure out where your life went astray. It is difficult to turn off the churn mode. You may find it difficult to be present in the moment, and you might develop sleep issues. Your emotions rise and fall as you succeed and fail. You experience frequent or chronic headaches, neurological disorders, sinus conditions, and disorders of the eyes or ears, diseases of the outer brain.

Your Third Eye is responsible for much of your physical health. This chakra is the energy center that governs the health of the neurological functions in your body. This will affect your body's ability to maintain proper metabolic functions, fight off infections, and sleep well. You might become sick frequently, develop problems with high blood pressure, or suffer from insomnia. If the Third Eye is completely blocked, you can also suffer from poor vision, sciatica, seizures, sinus issues, and migraines. Extreme cases of Third Eye problems can lead to blindness or stroke.

This sixth chakra is located in the middle of your forehead between your two physical eyes. This chakra is called your Third Eye because it is where you get your psychic vision from. This is your vision to see into the astral realm beyond the physical world. Your dreams will become a reality in the vision of your Third Eye. Some intuitives can see angels, spirit guides, ascended masters, and people that have crossed over. Your Third Eye is how you can see these things. When you activate this chakra, you can see beyond what you can see with your physical eyes. This allows you to open your consciousness to deeper understandings that expand your intuition. When this chakra is balanced, you possess the ability to reflect on your inner self and see the world and understand it.

CHAPTER 3
Benefits Of A Healthy Third Eye

Many people are already familiar with their Third Eye chakra. While your two normal physical eyes allow you to see the physical world all around you, the Third Eye is associated with the future, intuition, and in some matters, with the spirit world as well. While everyone possesses the Third Eye, everyone has not taken the effort to open it and perceive the world. Those who do will find it offers them several benefits in their daily lives.

Because this sixth chakra resides at the highest place in the body, it holds a particular position and power class. Once you open up your Third Eye, it will bring your other chakras into closer alignment. This ability allows you to create an internal harmony that helps you face the world as a whole entity and not someone out-of-step with themselves.

Unaligned energies will disrupt your sleep just as much as a physical problem will. Because your Third Eye chakra aligns with your brain, and more importantly, with your pineal gland, it greatly influences your sleep quality. This allows you to see your dreams more clearly and ensures a better quality of sleep. Your dreams are most easily interpreted through the lens of this particular chakra.

The Third Eye helps you see the world outside yourself, and it enables you to see into yourself and the world present inside your mind. With a strong Third Eye, you will be in touch with your inner creativity in methods that might have been difficult or sporadic in the past. Your imagination flows through this chakra, and keeping it open will allow you to tap into that part of yourself with greater ease than you've ever experienced before.

Opening your Third Eye will also bring you in-line with the flow of the universal energies all around you. You will join the flow, rather than the rocks trying to break up that flow. People and events will flow toward you. Opening your Third Eye makes you a magnet; other people will be drawn to you, even if they may not quite understand why.

Everyone has times where they feel stressed about something. Maybe it was those bills you had come that you weren't sure you could cover or a conversation with a loved one about a complicated topic. You may feel frustrated with your work, your family, or some other part of your life. Stress weighs on you, clouding your mind and making it difficult for you to see the solutions right in front of you. Opening your Third Eye will pierce the fog of frustration and anxiety, allowing you to see past beyond previously impossible problems. This clarity of mind will put doubts to rest and enable you to see solutions that you would never have seen with the chakra closed.

One of life's eternal struggles is trying to figure out where to go from where you are. Everyone has a destination, and no answer will work for everyone. However, by opening your Third Eye, you will see yourself and find your path. By visiting the hidden world around you, and the secret world within yourself, you will understand yourself, your needs, and your desires more thoroughly than you did before. This clarity will allow you to find the drive you need to achieve success.

If you know you are dreaming, but you can't wake up, and you can't change the course of what was happening, you are having a lucid dream. Some people can take control of their goals and maintain their agency during these nocturnal adventures. Lucid dreaming is easy for those who are in-tune with this chakra. Opening your Third Eye chakra is the key to astral travel and projection. Connecting your mind to the greater universe around you allows your spirit to leave your body and experience other astral planes.

An open Third Eye will make you more in-tune with yourself and with the universe around you. You will shed stress and find the solutions you need in your life. Achieving that goal requires effort, but once you finally manage to scale that summit, you will know the worth of your effort.

CHAPTER 4
Methods For Opening Your Third Eye

Energy radiates from everything in the universe. Energy flows around, through, and into all things large and small in the universe. Your cells give off power in various ways. The different sections in your body emit different types of energy that will depend on what their function is and where they are located. Several other channels are located in specific areas of the body that allow energy to flow out and at a constant pace. These are your chakras.

Your chakras spin to move energy out of your body and counterclockwise to pull fuel into your body. The individual chakra's current state will determine the order that the power will flow through your body. The opening and closing of the chakras are part of your body's internal defense mechanism. If you have a negative experience, then the chakra associated with that feeling will close so that it can block out that negative energy. You can close off a chakra by holding on to specific thoughts and feelings, which will cause the chakra to close to protect itself. When you fix your chakras and open them again, the energy is once again able to flow freely, and your energy levels will soon return to normal. Since every chakra is attached to a specific part of the nervous system and the endocrine system in your body, a closed chakra could lead to an energy deficiency that might cause a severe physical ailment if left for too long.

All of your chakras are equally important to your body in terms of balancing and flowing energy levels. An ideal situation is when all seven of your internal chakras are balanced, open, healed, and spinning at the proper frequency. Your body will find ways to move energy around. If one of your chakras is closed, the one next to it or its balancing chakra will work overtime to compensate for the deficiency. Your body wants a balance of energy, so it will find ways to make this happen. If one chakra is underperforming, it will cause another to overcompensate, and this will upset the natural balance of your chakras. You need to recognize when your chakras are imbalanced because over-performing is just as bad for your body as underperforming. Here is a list of the feelings you might experience when your Third Eye chakra is not healthy:

Underactive -- clinging to the past, closed off to new ideas, anxious, disconnected or distrustful of the inner voice, rigid in thinking, too reliant on authority, and fearful of the future

Overactive -- Lacking good judgment, unable to focus, out of touch with reality, prone to hallucinations

Physical Symptoms of Imbalance – Excessive nightmares, poor vision, headaches, seizures, and insomnia

Associated Organs and Endocrine Glands -- Eyes, brow, pituitary, the base of skull, biorhythms

This chakra is responsible for your intuition, thought, manifesting, perception, and reality. When this chakra has opened, a doorway to spiritual enlightenment is opened. When this chakra is balanced and clean, you will possess emotional balance, self-awareness, insight, strong intuition, and clarity. An unhealthy Third Eye will cause you to suffer from mood disorders, mental illnesses, paranoia, depression, anxiety, cynicism, and closed-mindedness. This chakra can quickly become damaged in childhood if you were raised in a close-minded family who taught you to be obedient and never question authority.

When this chakra is unhealthy, closed, or blocked, you will physically suffer from migraines, sinus problems, vision problems, and earaches. You will either be ungrounded and dreamy or opinionated and arrogant. You will be stubborn and find it difficult to be open-minded. You will find it challenging to like other people. You will indulge in superficial or trivial relationships because you will quickly dislike or distrust others. Your opinions of the world will be rigid and nearly impossible to change. Reality will not be clear to you, and you will have problems connecting to your soul or your deeper self. You might also be addicted to those things that make you feel pleasure like status, money, sex, shopping, drink, food, or relationships.

A balanced and open Third Eye Chakra will make it easier for you to be more objective in your opinions and less rigid in your beliefs. Your life will be more fluid and free-flowing, and this will allow you to be more spontaneous and creative. You will feel more compassion and wisdom, which will let you reach your mystical state of being much more quickly. This chakra might be a bit more difficult to heal since it involves a lot of soul growth.

It is essential to explore new points of view if you truly want to heal this chakra. This exploration will assist you in breaking the cycle of being close-minded and rigid in your beliefs. You will also be easily lost in delusion and fantasy if you are not grounded in reality. Try to work on being present in your everyday life and not allow your mind to wander off too far.

Get outside and enjoy some sunlight every day. This daily habit will help heal the Third Eye Chakra because it will help clear your mind. Use blue lotus, rosemary, passionflower, lavender, jasmine, basil, saffron, star anise, or mugwort herbs in cooking or as incense. These will also make delicious teas. Add to your diet more of the purple foods. The Third Eye Chakra enjoys purple potatoes, purple carrots, purple kale, purple cabbage, eggplant, raisins, figs, and blueberries, blackberries, dates, and prunes. Use Third Eye Chakra appropriate essential oils like vetiver, juniper, sandalwood, clary sage, frankincense, and patchouli. Amethyst, labradorite, kyanite, lapis lazuli, sapphire, and shungite crystal can be carried or worn. Work on your yoga poses, especially head-to-knee poses, child's pose, dolphin pose, and standing forward bend. Light a candle and set it three to four feet in front of you and stare at the flame. Keep your vision focused in a comfortable, natural way.

One of the reasons this chakra will be damaged is when you hold on to core beliefs that are limiting. Your core beliefs are the deep convictions you hold about you that make you feel self-loathing, insecurity, and fear. When you uncover those core beliefs that you keep hidden, you will open this chakra and keep it healthy. Try to be more self-aware, as this is a necessary skill that you need to develop. Keep a private journal of your deepest feelings and thoughts. Sit outside at midnight and stare at the full moon.

The main reason that your Third Eye Chakra becomes unhealthy or blocked is that you identify with the thoughts you think because you believe in them. Learn how to observe your thoughts without feeling they are the ultimate truth. Feelings and opinions do not have any meaning unless we give them meaning. And keep in mind that your dreams express your inner needs, fears, and desires. They are naturally rich in symbols that hold meaning for your life. You interpret your goals with the help of your Third Eye Chakra.

And always remember to tell yourself how well you are doing. Use positive affirmations as a guided meditation to heal and balance your Third Eye Chakra. Use phrases that begin with the words 'I see,' 'I trust,' or 'I create.'

Yoga for Opening the Third Eye

When it is open and awake, the Third Eye chakra causes a person to dream quite a bit, have a good sixth sense, and possess a fantastic intuition. But people who do not have an active Third Eye will allow other people to make decisions they should be making for themselves. They might be easily confused and rely on misleading information. An overactive Third Eye will cause a person to live in a world of dreams and imagination.

To awaken the Third Eye, sit with the legs crossed and the back straight and firm. Put the backs of the hands-on top of the knees with the index finger and the thumb touching gently, and the rest of the fingers relaxed. The eyes will be closed, and the concentration should be on the Third Eye chakra's health and how it will benefit your body and the mind. Clearly and softly speak the word "om." Think about how the Third Eye chakra can affect life and energy. Keep meditating until a clean, refreshed feeling comes over the body.

The pose to keep the Third Eye chakra opened and balanced will quickly open the mind to fresh thoughts and new learning when it is regularly practiced. It will assist in the development of instincts and the strengthening of intuition. The Third Eye chakra governs the remainder of the chakras' functions, so it is essential to keep it balanced.

Sit on the buttocks with the legs crossed. Lay the hands on the knees with the fingers facing up and the thumb and the index finger touch. Keep the spine straight and firm but not stiff. Balance your spine on top of the pelvis and do not lean either backward or forward. Exhale and let the shoulders relax, and then inhale and lift the spine. Relax the body with the eyes closed. Keep breathing slowly and rhythmically while holding the pose for at least a few minutes before releasing it.

Affirmations for Opening the Third Eye

Affirmations are beneficial when used to heal the chakras. Declarations will quite often have an immediate useful effect on a person's personal vibration and mood. The affirmation words are powerful enough to give energizing power to the spirit, soothing sufficient to heal the body, and direct sufficient to reprogram the mind.

Each chakra has its affirmations that can be spoken silently in mind or out loud. Use affirmations as statements to repeat affirmatively while feeling the positive emotion associated with that affirmation. Affirmations can be used daily and regularly or anytime when you think your chakras might need a bit of healing. Affirmations will only be effective if they are specific to the chakra, particular to the person, and phrased in the present tense. The words that correspond to the Third Eye chakra all deal with clarity of vision and thinking and enhanced creativity levels.

- I imagine
- I envision
- I see

The keywords for healing the Third Eye Chakra can be used in combination with other words as desired:

I imagine peace	I see clearly
I imagine freedom	I see possibilities
I imagine power	I envision power
I see potential	I envision potential
I imagine wealth	I imagine health
I have vision	I see far away
I imagine peace	I see beauty

These can also be used to complete longer affirmations as desired:

- I see my imagination open to all possibilities
- I envision my inner knowing accepting my psychic potential
- I see the light of my higher mind illuminating my life
- I expect a clear path toward my goals
- I imagine my mind filled with guidance and wisdom
- I know when things are going well in my world

- I imagine a healthy spirit, mind, and body
- I see beyond illusions to the truth of the matter
- I envision a bright and lively future filled with hope
- I picture my mind focused and clear
- I imagine my life going exactly the way it should
- I am imaginative and insightful
- I see great possibilities in my future life
- I envision a peaceful world well filled with joy and love
- I imagine the goodness in others and try to see it

Color for Opening the Third Eye

The chakras change with the changes in human emotion. Whatever color, they usually correspond to the human being's current physical, spiritual, and emotional state. There is a special connection between the state of the body and the colors of the chakras. The colors are fluid, and if the chakra is blocked, the energy can no longer flow through the body. This is because there is a distinct and intimate connection between the entire body and the body's components like the mind, the soul, and the spirit. The colors of the chakras invoke different emotions. When someone sees a rainbow, they envision a sense of calm after a storm. Other colors will invoke different feelings in the mind and the heart. Color is a universal language that is spoken by all people.

Indigo is the color of wisdom and deep knowledge. This color is most often associated with night and opening the door to the divine. Your senses are more awake at night and more open to receiving messages from other worlds. Indigo clarifies your sense organs – your ability to see, hear, and feel. The color indigo connects your mind to your Third Eye by creating a bridge that links your brain's two hemispheres together and links the span between life and death.

The energy of the indigo is the energy of significant change. This energy will become higher vibrations on the spiritual level. You will need to remain consciously connected to your friends and family, so you do not become disconnected from reality. The ease with which spiritual matters come to you now might leave you feeling ungrounded. You will begin to recognize patterns in your life. You will recall your past while you clearly see where you are going. Indigo physically relates to your pineal gland, your brain, nose, forehead, eyes, brow, the carotid nerve, and the pituitary gland. People who carry vital indigo energy wear a noticeable glow. Their eyes are bright and full of deep wisdom. This calming power brings healthy shifts that change and transform you.

Symbolic thinking gets its energy from indigo as it connects the material with the symbolic. The effortlessness of action associated with indigo means that you do not impose your own will or ego on the situation when you are in action. The action flows around you and through you, and your accomplishments will become effortless. Indigo is a color that brings calm and tranquility. You will know peace in your life. Since you are now connected spiritually with the divine, you will know that your life is going well and nothing will need to be changed.

Blocking this energy that comes from the color indigo and the Third Eye will lead to much physical impairment in your life. You might suffer from sadness and loneliness as well as depression, and you might also experience hallucinations and delusions. Your Third Eye chakra enhances and develops your consciousness. The workings of the Divine are apparent to you as you become one with the Universe.

This ability is available to everyone, whether you know it as your sixth sense, intuition, your inner voice, or your gut feelings. The process cannot be forced or stopped. It is always there. Listen to the feelings coming from your subconscious mind. That voice from within is stilled too often by the demands of an energetic world. But your intuition is always there, and you can access it at any time.

Your intuition gives you that strong feeling that something might be wrong, so do not dismiss it because you can't rationalize it, or you may regret it later. Use the color indigo to help you connect with your intuition. It will connect with the deepest parts of you, allowing you to access your instinct, gut feelings, or the sixth sense.

CHAPTER 5
The Third Eye Doorway To The Psychic World

Psychics are nothing more than individuals who possess abilities that go beyond the boundaries of the physical world. They can taste, sense, feel, hear, see, or have the power of intuition. The basic definition of psychic skills is processing data from intangible and tangible stimuli on a profoundly spiritual, physical, or emotional level. This explanation is a broad definition because psychic abilities vary significantly in application and intensity.

Most psychic abilities are initially developed in childhood. Children feel more, hear more, see more, and notice more. Children are naturally more psychic because, to them, everything is real, including spirits. They don't know that you shouldn't believe in things like that, so it is natural to think for them. As children grow older and are steered more in math and science and less in imagination and creativity, they lose their psychic abilities. As adults, they accept that the physical world is the only realm that exists. But your psychic skills are never truly lost, just buried, and you can quickly resume them with a bit of practice.

Psychic Readings with Mediums

A psychic reading is a particular attempt by someone to find out information through the discerning use of heightened mental abilities. It can also be determined by using your basic human senses of sight, smell, taste, sound, and touch. These are a form of prophecy—different types of psychic readings that can be done. The reading may or may not involve the use of tools, and the psychic who is doing the reading may possess more than one area of expertise. These readings include astrological readings, reading the aura, psychometry, palm reading, and reading tarot cards.

- Reading tarot cards does not explicitly require psychic abilities. It can be used as a psychic reading tool for cold readings.
- Runes are the letters of the alphabet that are cast onto a table and then read to try to see what path a problem will take or to see the course of future events in someone's life.
- Psychometry is a type of psychic reading where the reader will collect details about someone from touching one of their possessions. The reader will usually ask for an item

that is a favorite one of the person they need information on, believing that a favorite control will hold more of their energy.

- Palm reading involves foretelling someone's future by reading the curves, wrinkles, shapes, and lines on a person's palm. This gift does not require any psychic ability, but previous knowledge of the subject is needed.
- The ancient study of numbers and their effect on the lives of humans is numerology. It is a reading based on the values of the numbers in someone's birth date or the numbers corresponding to the letters in their names.
- Lithomancy involves reading the signs shown by stones or gems that are dampened and then tossed out to land in a pattern.
- Distant readings include any reading done from a distance, without any contact between the reader and the subject, and can be done by telephone, mail, email, or any number of communication methods.
- Crystallomancy uses a crystal ball to do readings for people, see the past for them, or perhaps know future events for them.
- Cleromancy uses different variations, but they all involve casting out a group of small objects and reading the message that is evident in their proximity to each other and their orientation and position in the group.
- Aura reading involves seeing and interpreting a person's aura based on its strength and pattern of colors.
- Astrology studies the relative position and movements of objects in the sky to determine terrestrial events and human affairs.

A medium is a person who performs the psychic reading and speaks to those in other worlds to collect information for those in the current physical plane. They receive messages from the spirit world in many different ways. Words and images are sometimes accepted as intuitive information through mental impressions. These images are then relayed to the living which seeks information. The medium might even hear auditory messages. Those who have passed on before are full of useful information that they like to impart to the living, and they use the services of mediums to bring that information to those who want or need it.

If a medium is conducting a séance, they will relay messages from the dead through their voices as they slip into a trance and allow the deceased person to take over temporarily.

Relaxation, Emptiness, and Meditation

Emptiness is just another way to look at experience, a way to perceive things. The raw data of mental and physical events will not be added to or subtracted by emptiness. It allows you to look at the events in the senses and the mind without wondering if there is something behind them. This thinking method is called emptiness because it is void of all of the suppositions that people usually add to events to make sense of them. It helps to make sense of the world we live in and the events around us. People create stories to fashion the view of the world as they see it. These views and actions do have their uses, but they also have downfalls. They can pull attention away from the reality of the world and our place in it. These stories and views that are created as explanations can interfere with understanding the world and solving its problems.

For example, imagine that you are meditating and suddenly remember the anger you feel toward a specific person. You will immediately identify this anger as belonging to yourself or say that you have angry feelings. You will then elaborate on this feeling to be worked into your general views of that person or your memories of every time they made you angry. The problem with this method is that all of these stories and viewpoints are full of anger and suffering. The more you involve yourself in these stories and feelings, the further you will move away from the offense's source and learn the actual cause. So you are unable to find the start of the problem, solve it, and move on.

When you choose to adopt the emptiness mode, you will neither react to the anger nor act upon it. Instead, you will merely view the offense as part of a series of events. You will see that anger itself has nothing to identify with and is not something to possess. When you can master the mode of emptiness, you will remove yourself from the emotion and go to the source. This removal allows you to isolate the event that caused the feeling to find a solution to the problem. This solution will enable you to see the truth in events, whether large or small. In this sense, all things are empty since they do not have the power to create a reaction in you. You will see the labels like 'my anger' and 'I am angry' do nothing but cause pain and stress because they are unnecessary and inappropriate.

Emptiness will require patience and practice to master. It involves training in discernment, concentration, and virtue. If you do not receive this training, your mind will remain in the mode that continues to create views and stories of the world. The idea is to focus on the quality of the intentions and perceptions present in your mind so that you can process them and move them into emptiness. Once the events are there, you will be able to lose all of your attachments to assumptions, stories, and views. Your mind will be empty of delusion, anger, and greed, and that will make it devoid of stress and suffering.

This emptiness of the mind will bring you to true wisdom, which is the true nature of the mind and not something you develop or acquire. To achieve this, many followers of Buddha practice Mahamudra meditation. This practice is an ancient tradition of wisdom that started in India. The philosophy aims to communicate the real nature of the mind, and the meditation part of the practice will bring that knowledge and experience rapidly. The tradition is best known for its simplicity. The idea behind this method is to be aware, relaxed, and genuine in all situations in life to appreciate and accept the person you are. You will not need to change your current style of energy to achieve this level of mind emptiness. This experience will point you in the direction of the mind's true nature and help you be completely joyful and free.

When you begin the Mahamudra meditation, you will need to realize that the mind's true nature is to be aware, luminous, and empty. You also need to understand that confusion will develop if you do not accept that nature. And you will also need to know that all the mind's experiences and expressions are naturally luminous and empty, free of any fixation or negativity. You will use the meditation to bring your mind to a complete realization of these truths.

To begin the practice of Mahamudra, you will first need to understand what Mahamudra meditation is. Then you will use that knowledge to do your way so that it will become your own experience. You can't use willpower, luck, or accident to realize the real nature of your mind. This knowledge is where Mahamudra meditation is needed. There are three distinct parts to Mahamudra meditation. The first part is a view of your world's basic reality and mind, and it is known as ground Mahamudra. The second part, path Mahamudra, is where you will learn and begin to use the practice of meditation. Then fruition Mahamudra will show you what the path of this meditation will lead you to. When all three parts are completed, you will have a total picture of the awakening journey known as Mahamudra.

When you can look inside with a steady and clear focus, you will see that your mind is open, spacious, and transparent. Your emotions and thoughts will be vivid, but you will not be able to see them, as they will disappear the moment you focus on them. When you realize the spaciousness of your own experiences, you will experience the emptiness part of the wisdom of emptiness. But your mind will not be full of only emptiness. Your mind will also hold the wisdom part of the emptiness wisdom, and this will make your mind awake and aware. The understanding of emptiness will bring you true enlightenment.

Mahamudra meditation is the process of being familiar with your mind as it exists now so that you can learn how to relax within it. When you first look into your mind, you will find that it is very poorly organized and usually wanders in all directions. Your first task will be to bring clarity and order to your mind. Your awareness will naturally become sharper and more precise when you are more mindful of how your thoughts work. Ultimately you will be able to inhabit an exact dimension of openness and presence as your mind expands and relaxes. The Mahamudra tradition's meditation will teach you how to see clearly and rest like your mind. Most people think that you need to concentrate on something to meditate, focus on one thing, and concentrate on it. Mahamudra meditation is not like that, but it is more about allowing your mind to relax and be transparent in its state. The best way to think of this is to plan to be mindful while relaxing and letting go of stress. It may feel stressful and unnatural at first, but it will be an easy way to meditate with time and practice.

Sit down somewhere that you are comfortable and where you will be free from distractions. Pay attention to how the seat feels under you and how your body feels in the center. Feel your soft breathing and the thoughts in your mind. Sit quietly and breathe for a few minutes, taking as long as you need to rid your mind of your thoughts. Look at the space directly in front of you with eyes aware of what they are seeing. Spend a few moments resting at this moment. Make your gaze like the space in front of you; nothing particular to focus on while you focus on the area. If any perceptions, emotions, or thoughts come to your mind, you should accept them without comment or judgment. Whether the thoughts and feelings are bad or good has no bearing on the situation. Just let your mind rest where it is.

The object of this meditation is to not focus on any one thing. Instead, you will focus on the awareness, clarity, and emptiness of your mind, for this will bring you to the true nature of your mind. While you are thinking about the void in your mind, think about the openness and space within. The radiance of the emptiness will bring clarity to your mind. Keep sitting there and staring into space until you begin to feel calm and rested. Then spend some time thinking about the clarity of your mind. Since all of your emotions and thoughts are your mind's natural expressions, then take the time to see them but do not feel them. If an angry idea pops into your mind, then acknowledge the thought but do not allow yourself to feel the anger. What you think about does not matter, but the way you think about it does matter. This feeling is the awareness of the mind.

Now rest your mind for a few minutes and let go of all thoughts and feelings. Stare into space before you while you bring your mind back into the present. Relax and feel the awareness of your mind as it sits in emptiness. Relax in this space for a few minutes before resuming your normal activities.

Psychic Sense with Automatic Writing

Automatic writing is the act of writing words when you are in an altered mental state like a trance when this state comes from somewhere outside of your conscious awareness, like the astral plane. Spiritualists and psychologists have differing opinions about how automatic writing happens. Some people believe that it is messages from angels and spirits, and others believe that it is merely the work of the person's unconscious mind. A third belief is that automatic writing emanates from the individual's subconscious mind, acting as a doorway to their Higher Self or their soul. You will reap many benefits from automatic writing when you take the time to perfect your abilities.

- You will better trust your intuition and instincts
- You will feel deeply understood and supported
- You might contact your spirit guides and know their opinions and perspectives
- Your intuition will be better developed and sharpened
- Your ability to make smart decisions will improve
- Your daily life will be more clear and concise
- You will better receive guidance directly from your higher power

And besides all of these benefits, automatic writing is a calming practice that will metaphorically and open your mind. Automatic writing is simple in its execution.

- Be ready with a way to write responses
- Ask a question you need an answer for
- Write the question down or type it out
- Allow your body and mind to relax
- Let the writing flow freely

Writing automatically does not take the time to stop and proofread or add punctuation where it is needed. Just write. So what you write may not be grammatically correct or even make sense in some parts, but write what your soul is thinking and feeling. Developing this ability will most likely not happen overnight. It will take some time and effort, so do not be discouraged and try to be patient.

The first time you attempt automatic writing, you might easily find that it comes to you and the words flow freely. And then you might discover that the second and subsequent attempts do not flow as easily. This momentary failure is a perfectly normal phenomenon. Whenever people try something new, they generally approach it with a clear, open mind without any expectations. Then they begin to build up mental baggage that gets in the way of their spontaneous revelation. If this happens to you, approach it again with a clear mind, without expectations, and you will most likely succeed. Follow the steps for automatic writing, and you will soon be an expert.

Think of something that you need help with. Especially if you struggle to hear your soul's thoughts in your daily life, automatic writing might be just the vehicle you need. Begin each new session with a clear mind, meditating first to relax if needed. Decide what you want an answer to at that moment, some burning question that is tearing you up inside and you need help with. You will get a better response if your item is charged with emotion. Address your question to a specific entity, such as your unconscious mind, soul, or spirit guide. Keep your question as simple as possible because that will make it easier for you to receive an answer. And if you have more than one question that needs answering, do more than one session.

Relax your mind before you begin. This relaxation is one of the most challenging steps for people today because life is hectic nowadays. But it is probably the most crucial step because you will not be able to be receptive to messages from your spirit guide if your mind is clouded. Your writing will come to you much more comfortable when your mind is empty of thoughts and still and calm. Clear your mind with the method that works best. Some possibilities you can use are yoga, visualization, mindfulness, deep breathing, and meditation.

Allow yourself to enter a light trance. Humans possess the ability to enter a spell quite easily. Being in a trance is a type of altered consciousness where your brain relaxes its normal processes. The spontaneous flow of information will come to you in your automatic writing when your mind is relaxed. Suppose you need assistance to enter a trance state. In that case, you can try self-hypnosis, guided meditation, doing repetitive tasks, deep breathing exercises, repeating mantras as chants, or listening to music.

When the information begins to flow, do not stop it. As soon as you feel you are prepared, you can start to write. Your words might not make sense at first, but that is okay. If you can't understand what you are writing, that is a good sign because it means you are tapped into something that works far past your thinking mind. You might also be tempted to judge what you are writing but try not to. If you see that your thinking mind is trying to become involved, gently put it back into its relaxed state. You might need to repeat the exercise you used to get into the trance, which is normal, especially in the beginning. If you are not used to writing, that might take some getting used to, but it will come in time. And be sure to give yourself as much time as you need to be able to express the information that you need.

Don't try to interpret the information until you are finished writing. You will know when your session of writing is completed. You will abruptly stop writing, or your thoughts will begin to taper off gradually. Once you feel you are done for that session, it is time to analyze your writing. Look first for any coherent thoughts or sentences in the writing or any word you have often used. If you find your writing confusing, just put it aside and come back to it later. And if your writing makes absolutely no sense, then that might be a sign that you need to ask a different question.

The way you feel when you are writing is the best way to tell if you receive guidance from your soul. You may feel frantic and emotionally charged, or you may feel light and spacious. If your writing becomes heavy and desperate, it usually means that your writing is coming from your emotions or your mind. And review what you have written to determine where the words are coming from. Thoughts that come from your soul will always feel and sound clear even if the words you wrote are a bit garbled and nonsensical. Thoughts that are coming from your mind will often be vague, critical, or disjointed.

Psychic Power with Extrasensory Perception (ESP)

Extrasensory perception, also known as ESP, is the reception of information with the mind. This ability includes retrocognition, precognition, clairvoyance, psychometry, telepathy, and intuition. There is also the phenomenon of second sight, where a person can know things that are not readily available to the five senses, but they may receive a vision or otherwise see this information. ESP is the sixth sense of human beings. People often think that the activities that some call ESP are mere coincidence. You might think of a particular person, and then they come to visit.

Another example is when two people lock eyes simultaneously, as though each was thinking of looking at the other. The information traded in events involving ESP is felt in the heart, the soul, and the gut feeling that you often think. ESP is not held to any boundaries of space and time. It will allow you to see into the future, know the thoughts that others are thinking, and even manipulate physical objects. There are many different ways to experience ESP, but the most common ones for people to share are the six that follow.

Mediumship – This is a form of ESP that makes many people turn away. It involves communicating with dead people and channeling their spirits to receive messages for those waiting here on earth. Depending on the medium's intentions and the receiver of the message, this channeling can take the form of different types of ESP like clairvoyance.

Clairvoyance – This is the ability to see information about an event in the future, present, or past, including seeing things about a location, scene, person, or object by using only ESP. This power can happen unintentionally, but it is usually most vital when you are practicing meditation. There are different forms of prophecy. The ability to receive information through the human sense of taste without actually eating anything is clairgustance. If your sense of smell psychically brings you impressions of things, then you have clairvoyance. The ability to receive information through hearing using your sixth sense and psychic abilities is clairaudience. Clairsentience lets you feel the emotions and sensation that another person feels without being stimulated externally. This ability often goes along with paranormal activities, such as when you can feel the coldness emitted by a ghost.

Telekinesis (or psychokinesis) – This gives you the ability to directly and physically affect an object without ever touching it yourself. You will use only the energy of your mind and not any physical energy.

Retrocognition – This ability is the direct opposite of precognition. This ability gives you the power to see into the past, and usually into the distant past. You will be able to recognize events, places, and people from a past that you were never a part of. Another aspect of this kind of ESP is déjà vu, where you feel your recent experience was an experience you took part in before at some time in the past. People with this type of ESP are often able to furnish minute details of past places and people they should never have been able to see or know.

Precognition – This form of ESP is the ability to see directly into the future. If you possess this, then you will know information about scenes, events, places, and people before the experience even happens.

Telepathy – This is the ability that allows you to know what other people are thinking. If you have this ability, you can communicate with other people without speaking or writing words. You need no different sense to share besides the power of your mind.

The Eight Limbs of Mind Yoga

If you find yourself experiencing negative emotions or thoughts, that might be a sign that you need to grow, learn, and stretch emotionally. This experience is where mental yoga comes into play. Like in physical yoga, you might need to experience some discomfort to reach the place you want to be. Three ideas make up the practice of mental yoga. You will first need to accept that the emotions you feel are normal and a natural part of life on earth. You will feel regret, anger, sadness at different times in your life. If you accept these experiences and emotions instead of eliminating them or controlling them, you will feel better mentally. Use your innate sense of curiosity to learn from your adverse reactions while you view them without judging yourself or your responses. Your interest will engage your sense of logic. This reasoning will allow you to learn from your reactions and use that knowledge to intelligently create the next steps to lead you closer to your goals. And when your mind is finally free of the fight to stress about or resist your natural emotional states, then you will easily be able to commit to behaviors and actions that will help you achieve your desires.

Study the ancient texts that speak of the tradition of yoga. You will see that the actual physical poses are not the basis of traditional yoga practice. It is easy to think of yoga as a form of exercise for flexible people and like to do combinations of contortions. But the real gifts that yoga will give you will come from the spiritual, psychological, and mental aspects much more than the physical ones. Yoga is not an exercise but a way of life. Real yoga means treating your body and mind well all of the time, keeping your mental balance and physical balance, and keeping a healthy mindset.

The eight limbs of Ashtanga yoga will teach you much about the philosophy of yoga. These principles are the guidelines for living an enlightened life and are part of yoga's most authoritative and oldest teachings. The eight limbs deal with integrity, self-discipline, yoga poses, controlling your breathing, cultivating internal awareness, concentration, meditation, and transcending the self. You need to achieve the first seven if you want to achieve the eighth one. Begin by focusing on the first limb, where you learn to be moral and act all of the time ethically, not just when it is convenient. You will learn to practice restraint, refrain from coveting or stealing, practicing honesty, and avoiding violence.

Be gentle with yourself, even if it seems like selfishness. There is nothing wrong with putting your own needs first, at least some of the time. Indeed, you will not be able to take care of the needs of others properly if your own is not being met. When you are aware of your needs and confident and secure in yourself, you will bring more to the world. You need to learn to acknowledge your own needs, even if all you need is a break. Be honest with your feelings. This examination is the purpose of practicing mental yoga, learning to take care of you first in an elementary but non-selfish way. Mental yoga will benefit you in ways you might never have thought of.

You will be more prepared to deal with the issues you face daily. No one else can change you, and you are the only one who can control your behavior and actions. You need to own your peculiarities and not blame yourself for having them.

You will become more aware of qualities you might not have known that you possess. Using the dark and light powers in yoga will help you recognize those qualities you might not realize in yourself. You will become more mindful of yourself. Those random places in your body where you are holding little knots of energy, muscle tightness, or tension are the places where your emotional or psychological life has backed up and is stagnating. Like yoga poses to stretch your muscles and release physical tightness, mental yoga will release mental and emotional tightness. Practice working on your mind and soul to change yourself or accept that you can function well with faults and weaknesses.

Your romantic relationships will be so much more fulfilling. Living a life where you are more at peace with yourself and more relaxed will allow you to be the same way with your partner. You will be able to give away more love when you feel more love for yourself. You will be less reactive to small annoyances.

Your sense of self will significantly improve. Mental yoga will allow you to build a sense of trust in yourself. Physical yoga makes you want to exercise more and eat healthily. Mental yoga will make you more rooted in your sense of self. You will be more confident and mentally balanced. You will have energetic willpower and courage. You will have nothing to hide and nothing to prove.

Your level of anxiety will significantly diminish. Without mental yoga, you probably spend a great deal of time planning to fight or flee. With mental yoga, you will move from the more reactive state to the more relaxed state that will allow you to feel less anxiety. This relaxation will calm your nervous system and will enable you to feel more peace and love for yourself and others.

The more you can be confident in your gifts and grounded in yourself, the more you will resist the world's temptations to conform to society and its demands. You will know yourself and what you want and need, and you will not be afraid to pursue your dreams.

CHAPTER 6
Consciousness Of The Third Eye

Having an awareness of your mental and physical awareness is known as consciousness. Not all of the forms of understanding are the same. Besides the number of things that can affect these states of attention, you will find that all forms of awareness are the same. Like a stream of flowing water, the human being's consciousness is always flowing smoothly while it is continually changing.

The Third Eye States of Consciousness

Human consciousness can be altered in several ways. Anytime you question how the mind works, analyze a dream you had, or felt surprisingly energetic in the morning, you were relating your life to your consciousness. Some people wake up vigorous and ready to face the day, only to fall into a slump in the middle of the afternoon. Other people drag themselves through the day until the sun goes down, and then they are wide awake and ready for action. Circadian rhythms dictate the fluctuation of your energy levels throughout the day. These rhythms also play an essential part in your consciousness. Sometimes referred to as your internal clock, these rhythms' patterns will help determine your physiological states when you understand how the environmental and biological conditions will give you much information about how the circadian rhythms will affect your conscious states.

Sleep is a state of consciousness. For thousands of years, scholars, scientists, and researchers have been fascinated by sleep and its study. It has been theorized that there are several significant reasons why human beings sleep. Sleep is essential for the restoration and repair of your body. It will keep your mind functioning correctly in good health. It is also necessary for the restoration and revitalization of your physiological processes. Protein synthesis and cell division increase while you are asleep, which is even more evidence that humans need sleep to repair their minds and bodies. Your body needs defined periods of inactivity and activity to learn how to conserve energy. Humans also sleep to consolidate the information they have received while they are awake. Besides processing information obtained during the day, the brain will also take time to get ready for the next day. A lack of sleep will have a seriously detrimental effect on your ability to recall information. Another reason for rest is that it allows the brain to cleanse itself. During your normal daily activities, your brain releases waste products. During sleep, the brain's fluid level increases, and this fluid helps to wash out the waste products.

Another state of consciousness is the dream state that you will achieve while you are asleep. People dream of replaying the events of the day or of imagining what could be in their lives. And the brain spends a reasonable amount of time trying to make sense of the brain's activity while the body is asleep. There are specific characteristics that dreams will have. The emotions that you might experience in your dreams will often be acute, painful, and quite intense. A common thread in dreams is something terrifying, like being attacked or falling. Another common theme of dreams is finding yourself in an intensely embarrassing situation, like making a speech and finding yourself naked. If the emotion is strong enough, you might wake up in the middle of it in an attempt to escape the feelings. Sometimes your dreams are full of inconsistencies and ambiguities that can lead you to experience very bizarre dreams. One of the characteristics of plans is that they usually don't observe any laws regarding people, places, or time, and they often make no sense.

When you are dreaming, you accept the odd content of your dream without question. The strength of your perceptions and emotions feeds the unquestioning acceptance of the dream state. All of the events that happen within the dream seem to belong in the dream; even if they are out of place or illogical at the time, your mind will tell you that they belong in the dream. If you can recall the dream when you wake up, your logical awake mind will find the events strange and challenging to explain. And you will often experience strange feelings in your dreams. Some of the more common feelings are not being able to control your body, the inability to move, or the sudden feeling of falling.

During the dream, you will feel that your memory is more intense than usual, but when you awaken, you will often find that your memory of the dream fades rapidly as soon as you wake up. Some people are acutely unaware of dreams' characteristics and may not be aware of how common many of the traits are.

Your unconscious mind is a treasure trove of memories, urges, thoughts, and feelings that lie outside your conscious awareness. When you are unconscious, most of the feelings you have, like conflict, anxiety, and pain, will feel unpleasant or unacceptable while you are in that state. Your unconscious mind will continue to influence your experience and behavior, even when you are not aware of the influence. Think of the unconscious mind as looking like an iceberg. The small area that you see above the water level represents your conscious mind, and the large chunk that you can see below the surface of the water is your unconscious mind. Those things that are characterized by your conscious awareness are nothing more than the tip of the iceberg. The remainder of the information in your mind lies underneath the surface. And while this information might not be readily available to you consciously, it will influence your behavior. All of your basic urges and interests are contained in your unconscious mind. Your unconscious mind also holds the instincts that you have related to survival and those thoughts that are not usually socially acceptable, like aggression. You can use dream interpretation and free word association exercises to bring forth those ideas that are locking in your unconscious mind.

Third Eye Etheric Vision

The etheric body is the subtle body, the essence of the soul, or the aura of a person. This etheric body emits a low level of electricity known as an electromagnetic field. It surrounds the person in layers of colors that correspond to the different elements of your emotional, spiritual, mental, and physical health. People who can see these layers surrounding people have an etheric vision.

Before you can see an aura, you will need to be able to sense the atmosphere. An excellent way to begin developing your etheric vision is to pay attention to how you feel when you are around other people. Make a mental note of the gut reactions or physical sensations that you think. See if other people make you feel excited, calm, nervous, angry, or any other emotion you can think of. You might label that person with a color that you think fits them best. Someone sad might make you think of the color blue, while someone happy and upbeat might make you feel about the color yellow. As you become better at judging the other person's aura, identifying them with colors will be more comfortable.

Since the photosensitive cells in the sides of your eye are more robust than the ones in the center part of your eye, you will need to work on developing your peripheral vision. The photosensitive cells are a kind of neuron that mammals have in their retinas. They are especially sensitive to the presence or absence of light, so they are excellent receptors for a person's aura. Spend time paying attention to objects that are just outside of your direct line of sight. Don't cause yourself unnecessary anxiety while doing this by trying to strain or stress. Keep your breathing regular and take your time. As your peripheral vision becomes more assertive, you will see auras than you did before more easily.

The colors in a person's aura are among the most critical aspects of a person's aura. One of the best methods to employ for improving your ability to read the auras when you see them is to read and understand the colors in the aura. An easy way to practice this is to tape pieces of construction paper at different places in a neutrally colored and lit room. Then concentrate on the colors and the feelings that the colors of the paper give you. The most significant part of reading shades in an aura is knowing how those colors make you feel because, with the etheric vision, you will use all of your senses and not just your ability to see.

Now you are ready to begin practicing on people. Ask a trusted friend to help you and always get their permission first. Have your friend stand fifteen to twenty inches in front of you and in front of a neutral wall in color. Now stare at the wall and not your friend and see if you can sense their aura with your etheric vision. Now look at your friend gently, but do not stare, and use your telepathy to ask her aura to show its colors to you. Make a note of any colors that you see and anything else that comes to your vision. When you can see your friend's aura, ask them to move slightly to see if you can still detect their aura. Now do something to change their mood and see if the colors in the aura change.

Once you have mastered seeing the aura of your friend, then you should practice on yourself. Because your aura is always more challenging to see, this is one of the easiest ways to strengthen your etheric vision and your other psychic abilities. Start by relaxing in a quiet place. Clear your mind of any distractions. Before you begin, either think or say your intention to access and view your aura. Quickly rub your palms together to activate the energy between them. Keep doing this until you feel as though they are attracted to each other like two magnets. Now focus your attention between your palms and see if you can see the energy there. This is your aura. See if you can see the magnetic waves or any of the colors of your aura.

There are photographic methods that will enable you to see someone's aura, but that will not help you develop your etheric vision powers. Simply keep practicing until you are easily able to do it. Keep your attitude positive while practicing because any negative emotion will get in the way of your ability to see auras.

The Third Eye and Temporal Vision

The human field of vision is the area of space that a person can see simultaneously. It refers to the field of vision that you can see peripherally without moving your head or eyes. If an object near you emits light that you can see, then that object is considered in your field of vision. Temporal vision refers to the amount of time it takes you to see something instead of a spatial image, which is how much you will see in one glance. Temporal vision also refers to seeing things with your material eye instead of seeing things with your spiritual eye. Earthly vision will only come from the human eye and never from the Third Eye.

Another critical component for temporal vision is that it pays attention to time, logic, and sequence. While you are developing your spiritual eye, you will need to use your earthly imagination. You will need to practice seeing things in real-time before seeing and feeling them spiritually. You have the sensors you need to develop this method of seeing. When you link your Third Eye with your visual cortex, you will see with your heart and your mind.

Your physical eyes are useless for those times you need to see the invisible world's energy and spirit. Your retinas will only register a thin band in the energy of the electromagnetic spectrum. Physical eyes do not see infrared light or ultraviolet light, and these are two of the bands that your skin readily responds to. Imagine the optic nerve as the cable that transmits images to the screening room in the back of your head. It is not able to discern electromagnetic fields. Your visual cortex can translate energy into live images. The ability to see power is already in place in your brain. If you want to see the images you were always meant to see, you will need to let your visual cortex take control and change the signal's source.

Third Eye Spirituality and Mysticism

As concepts mysticism and spirituality have always been slightly difficult to define since so much of their understanding will depend on your perspective. All of the significant religions feature some form of mysticism, which has long been regarded as how you will reach the inner dimensions of your life, a place where you will achieve unity with the Divine Being of your choice. Spirituality is a concept with more possible meanings. Sometimes it is associated with those religious traditions that emphasize the growth of your inner life. This spirituality will include the ability to develop a spiritual experience that is deeper and more meaningful. In recent years the development of spirituality has moved farther away from the religious aspect and more toward the idea of achieving virtuous and ethical behavior as being normal.

As part of everyday life, mysticism is performing activities based on faith as you complete your regular daily activities. It is the search for and the pursuit of a relationship with a higher being. The desire is that this relationship will bring spiritual truth to your reality. Someone who helps you to achieve this religious experience is known as a mystic. The differences in psychological, social, and religious traditions will express how this term is defined. The mystic will also help you describe the communion that you were able to achieve with your Higher Power. Beliefs like these are considered to be somewhere beyond the intellectual or perceptual mind. Mysticism is spiritual, but it is not spiritualism as it is now defined. Mysticism is more of an organic process that includes the perfect union with the love of your Higher Power. The exact definition of mysticism will depend on the religious tradition that is defining it.

While mysticism is generally thought of as having religious connotations, it is not reserved simply for the spiritual element. The ability to become a mystic is an inborn trait, and there are two possible paths that you can follow if you desire this position. You can perform different activities that will bring you closer to communion with your Higher Power. These activities include meditation, which is one of the best ways to open your reception to messages from the Divine. Some people experience voices or visions because mysticism has been thrust upon them after any unexplained or traumatic experience. The traumatic experience does not need to be something wrong because anything outside of your normal realm of daily activities can be traumatic to your system.

Spirituality is the solitary adventure that your soul will take as it seeks for truth and morality in your life. Spirituality has nothing to do with worldly interests. And while spirituality is a broad term, it becomes even more comprehensive when defined by the different groups that seek spirituality. New age followers, Native Americans, polytheists, monotheists, and many others seek spirituality and determine what spirituality is. In all groups, it will deal with developing the master of the body, which is the spirit.

You can't define spirituality for anyone besides yourself because it involves deeply personal, subjective experiences. It generally includes a feeling of being connected to a more extensive power than you personally, and it affects your search for meaning in your life. As a human experience, spirituality is universal. You might describe your spirituality as transcendent or even sacred if that is what it means to you personally. It will bring a deep sense of being alive and connected to something larger than you are.

While you might define spirituality in terms of your religious experience, the act of being spiritual is much larger than being religious. While the two concepts are not the same thing, they are not that different, and they can overlap in your life. Spirituality will lead you to seek a better path for your personal life, more meaning in your life, and a way to feel connected to others. Mysticism will lead you to seek truth in life, the difference between right and wrong, and a desire to follow certain rituals that will bring you closer to your goal. Both of these disciplines look for the awe in ethics, reflective thinking, mental and emotional comfort, and a belief in something that will watch over you and help you on your journey.

Third Eye Psychic Visions

The word clairvoyance comes from two French terms that mean a clear vision. A person who has the powers of prophecy is known as a clairvoyant. It is the ability to get information from a physical event, location, person, or object. There is also the ability for remote viewing, which is the ability to perceive current events that happen outside of the range of a person's normal perception; retrocognition, which is the ability to see events that occurred in the past; and precognition, which is the ability to predict or perceive events that have not yet happened. All people are born with extraordinary psychic abilities, and they will appear in different people in different manifestations. You will know that you are clairvoyant if you can do any or all of the following:

- If you can paint pictures using words and feelings, or if spoken or written words give you the ability to create an image in your mind

- If you have vivid dreams that you can still recall once you are awake, or if you have recurring dreams that mirror events in your life
- If you see things just out of your range of view, and when you look to check, there is nothing there
- If you have dreams or visions that tell about future events
- If you feel an unusual awareness of the area of your third eye or if the middle of your forehead starts tingling

When you are a child, your pineal gland is functional and fully operational, and it is much larger than it will be when you are an adult. As you age, your pineal gland shrinks due to a loss of spiritual awareness. You will need to give your third Eye attention and love if you want to keep your psychic abilities intact. If you regularly use your Third Eye, you will enjoy oneness with the Universe. The main focus of many spiritual practices in achieving this oneness is to increase your empathy for your fellow human beings. At the same time, you release your worries and dissolve inherent stress. There are signs that you can follow that will let you know when your Third Eye is coming open and beginning to function

- As your Third Eye starts to open and you become more aware of yourself and your abilities, you will see that you are more loving, forgiving, and calmer. These changes in your temperament will help you move away from the processed foods that impact your Third Eye's health.
- You will become more sensitive to light as your Third Eye begins to open. This sensitivity means that you are beginning to see the world in a new, brighter light. The hues of colors will also appear to you as more rich and vivid. Anything related to light and vision will be expanded and heightened.
- As you become more accustomed to the presence of your spiritual self, you will begin to enjoy the benefits of the new view you have of the world. Your spiritual powers and intuition will guide you to make life choices guaranteed to make you healthier.
- You might begin to feel different sensations in your forehead, like a growing feeling of pressure between your eyes. Do not let this feeling worry you because it is entirely natural. You might also feel warmth in your forehead.
- You might also begin to feel experiences of an increased ability to see events before they happen. You may feel nothing more than a slight tugging in your stomach. Let this

feeling guide you forward, and do not overlook it. You will have an easier time allowing this feeling to show you how you realize it is totally within your control.

- As your power grows more substantial, you will be able to see and know more than other people know. You will be able to spot untruths easily. Your thoughts will be clear and will flow easily.
- The final sign of the opening of your Third Eye is so subtle that many people never notice. Your sense of self will increase so that you feel you are part of the fabric that makes up the Universe and not just a mere human with dislike, likes, and interests. You will begin to achieve the life that you always wanted as you rely more on yourself due to your increased sense of self.

It can be confusing or even scary in the beginning if you are not prepared to deal with the signs of having an active Third Eye. During this time, your greatest asset will be calming activities and meditation that will allow you to have a deeper connection to your spiritual self. No matter what path you choose, these manifestations are there to help you and should not be feared.

The Tunnel of the Third Eye

Many people trying to open their Third Eye have reported strange sensations during different learnings they are doing. One of the most common is the vortex that people often see while they are meditating. This vortex is a perfectly normal phenomenon and nothing to worry about. Seeing this vortex is something to be desired. This vortex is the tunnel that will lead you to the places your Third Eye will show you. It holds power to transport you to other realms.

When your Third Eye is open, and the vortex appears to you, it will look something like a golden halo of bright light that has spinning effects whirling around it. The center of the vortex is the tunnel you want to see; the tunnel will help you on your travels. If you do not know the tunnel or the vortex right away, just be patient because some people require more time to see it than other people. Your goal is to enter the tunnel when it opens to you since it will be your passageway to the astral world. Since your goal is to find this vortex with your fully-opened Third Eye, you can do things to make it happen.

- If you try to force the vortex to happen, it never will, so be patient and let it happen in its own time

- Follow your standard methods and plans for meditating, as long as these are working for you, and if you need to make changes, don't be afraid to do so
- Don't put your focus on the physical area of your Third Eye but try to focus on a point in the distance, something in the center of your vision, and set your concentration on this point
- Over time your consciousness will gradually increase, and your focus will naturally be drawn to this point, but let it happen in due course and never try to force the sensation
- Meditating to open your Third Eye and enter the tunnel is just like any other practice of meditation; it takes time and technique, and will become more comfortable with time and practice

You might not be seeing the tunnel or even the vortex, but you may have begun seeing an array of colors while you are meditating. This image is an indication that you are beginning to open your Third Eye and taking positive steps toward spiritual awakening. The color you see while you are meditating will correspond with your chakras, the energy centers inside your body. If you see more or less of one particular color, this might be a sign that your body's area is ailing and needs assistance.

Telepathic Awareness

When you can receive feelings or thoughts over distances from another person, this is known as telepathy. Telepathic awareness grows with the deepening ability of the Third Eye. When you use telepathy, you will not use any of the five basic senses of smell, taste, touch, sound, and sight. People who already have a close relationship are much more likely to be able to use telepathy. One example of this is the bond between twins who always seem to know what the other one is thinking no matter how far apart they are physically. This kind of relationship can be acquired with anyone if the conditions are right.

Telepathy is inborn in everyone, but communicating this way will require a conscious effort on your part. Learning how to use telepathy prevents many people from being able to since they approach skepticism and a lack of awareness. Another significant factor in people rejecting the idea of telepathic communication is the general view of society. Simultaneously, some cultures will embrace telepathy, just as many will reject the idea as nonsense.

You will be better able to communicate telepathically if you are in a relaxed state. Meditation is one good way to learn to relax and open your mind. When you are in the proper condition, your body will relax, your mind will open, and your spirit will be receptive to sending and receiving others' messages. Continue working to strengthen your ability to communicate with others this way and never listen to those who try to prevent you from doing so. When you try to send a message to someone telepathically, try to use great detail to envision the other person. Imagine that they are standing in front of you and having a conversation with you. You will not get instant results, so be patient while you are learning.

While you are sending your message, you should begin to feel that your message is being received. When you think of this, you should stop trying to send your message. You might think that you imagine things when you first begin receiving messages from other people. Listen to these thoughts and remember them, but keep in mind that they are perfectly normal. You will receive communications in various ways. You will experience desires, images, thoughts, emotions, and feelings. Some people can even receive and send messages while they are asleep.

You will relate to people with greater understanding and on a higher level once you begin to connect with other people using telepathy. This ability will have a serious effect on your relationships. And communicating telepathically is a more efficient method of communication. It is instantaneous, free, environmentally friendly, and the location is not essential as telepathy works anywhere. You will easily contact anyone, anywhere, at any time. You will also block other people from sending messages to you if you do not want to communicate with them. This communication will take a bit more effort to learn, but it is well worth the effort.

CHAPTER 7
Astral Beings And The Third Eye

Your Third Eye is a light that you will see when your eyes are closed, visible there behind the darkness. Through the morning of your spiritual vision, you will be able to look into other realms. The Third Eye reflects cosmic energy as it enters your body and helps to sustain you. This cosmic energy enters you through your Third Eye.

You will see that the spiritual eye looks like a halo of golden light surrounding a circle of deep blue. Centered in the blue circle is a five-pointed, silvery-white star. If this symbol appears in your meditation, you should concentrate on the star in the blue field center. While you are focused, the golden halo will gradually expand and stretch into a tunnel. If you allow yourself to pass into the tunnel, you will be entering the light of the astral world. The blue light will form a tunnel that will lead you into cosmic consciousness. As you pass through the star in the center, you will then enter the astral world beyond creation.

Other Worlds

Parallel worlds do exist, and they are detectable because they interact with our world here on Earth. It isn't easy to test these other worlds' actual presence, but those who believe in them believe entirely. There is compelling evidence to verify the existence of these parallel worlds. One of these pieces of evidence comes from the world of quantum physics, which theorizes that every one of the possible outcomes of any situation does happen. Still, they occur in different Universes because only one result of a case can occur in each Universe. This would necessitate an infinite number of parallel worlds to allow this theory to be possible, and this idea is just as valid as any other explanation. As of now, no observations or experiments have wholly overridden the possibility. The second theory comes from the world of physics and the idea of the multiverse. While it is speculated that the Universe that we live in began with the Big Bang, it is also supposed that the Big Bang was not the beginning that we have always assumed that it was. The theory is that cosmological inflation happened before the Big Bang, and where the inflation ended, the Big Bang happened. This inflation did not end everywhere at once, so where it did not end, other Universes would have been created after our Universe was created.

And once inflation begins, it is impossible to stop it, and when inflation ends in a particular place, there will be a Big Bang that will create a new Universe.

While there is no concrete proof that parallel worlds exist, there is also no concrete proof that they don't exist. These other worlds can share the matter with our Universe. And there is evidence that shows that a parallel world is not only possible but also probable. Recent radio wave studies have demonstrated radio waves below the polar ice cap, in an area that should have been frozen since the beginning of time. This evidence goes right along with other astrophysical quandaries like black holes and pulsars.

Traveling the Astral Planes

Astral travel goes by many different terms, depending on the tradition or religion that is referring to it. The Hindu body of bliss, Tantric spiritual body, the Christian experience of other heavens, Taoist diamond body, Egyptian ka, Buddhist light body, energy body, dream body, or astral body can be known as the Hindu body of bliss. All these terms mean the same thing: astral travel. The human being's standard design includes the subtle body, and it is the subtle body that astrally projects and is active during lucid and unconscious dreaming. Out-of-body experiences are usually the combination of dreaming and astral projection. When the subtle body is cultivated, it will survive the physical body as a consciousness model. Part of the spiritual energy training paths for developing the subtle body is lucid dreaming and astral projection.

Out-of-body experiences can be involuntary or intentional. Depriving yourself of food or water, illness, or trauma can all trigger an out-of-body experience. Good opportunities for purposeful astral experiences are lucid dreams. The adventure begins with the knowledge of consciously observing the body after leaving it. Awareness can be directed to activities or locations of your choice with some lucidity and practice.

The subtle body or the astral body has long been acknowledged as truly existing. Esoteric techniques for healing were developed from the recognition of the celestial body. Distance healers, followers of the Reiki method, and energy healers are familiar with these techniques and use them in modern times, working specifically with the energetic body.

The rational soul and the physical body are linked together by an intermediate body of light known as the astral body. The middle world between Earth and Heaven is the astral plane. When your celestial body leaves your body to travel the astral plane, astral travel is known. Accounts of astral travel are widely documented. These travels are usually described as the journey of the soul into other realms.

People who practice astral projection validate the existence that there is life after your physical body's death. They describe the experience as finding themselves present and aware of themselves outside of their physical body. They can taste, smell, touch, hear, and see. You cannot dismiss the idea that your physical life is nothing more than a moment away from the spiritual plane of existence. A switch is activated inside of you when you are engaged in conscious astral projection, sleeping, or deep in meditation. This switch is also known as your pineal gland, which is necessary for opening your Third Eye, which helps bring you closer to the possibility of astral travel. Chemicals released from the pineal gland cause your soul to leave your body during near-death experiences, when your soul is leaving your body at the point of death, or when you are sleeping or meditating, and the soul goes for astral travel.

You have no control over what your soul does while you are sleeping because that is when your subconscious owns your soul. There are benefits to consciously practicing astral travel. It will take you beyond the limitations of the rational and the physical. Many people experience the inner blooming of their spiritual being and a profound shift in their astral senses. They enjoy a complete transformation of their perspective of themselves as physical and spiritual beings. After astral travel, these people use a greater consciousness during life activities because they are secure in knowing that they are more than just mere physical beings doomed to live short, boring lives.

There are many benefits to astral travel. It will enrich your soul and your life. You will have a better understanding of the spirit world and your place on the astral plane. Your religious limitations will shatter. Any restrictions you had previously put on your life and your beliefs will end when you begin astral travel.

Out of Body Experiences

The experience where your soul leaves your body is astral projection or out of body travel. Your soul is free of your physical body, and it can travel independently of your physical body. This travel is not the same experience when someone dies, and their soul leaves their body permanently. Astral travel allows your soul to leave you and roam free while you remain alive, and then your soul will rejoin your body. Astral travel is an old idea that is present in many cultures around the world. It will sometimes happen during meditation or while a person is dreaming.

Western thought says that the astral body is a form of light that links the soul to the body's physical part. The astral plane is composed of stars and lights, as it is the plane located between Earth and Heaven. The stars and planets of the astral plane are populated with spirits, demons, and angels. The celestial body, also known as the subtle body, and the planes of existence the subtle bodies are associated with, form an esoteric system of the cosmic phenomenon. These planes of reality and the heavenly bodies are often pictured as a series of circles winding around and over. A particular type of celestial body will travel to each realm.

In the Biblical world, the subtle body links to a psychic cord's physical body. It is taught that the silver cord should never be entirely loose from either the subtle body or the physical body. In ancient Egypt, the soul, the subtle body, has the power to hover over the physical body and watch it. In China, the Taoists believe that the two forms of the person, the subtle body and the physical body, can leave the other to perform different acts and then come back together later.

You can prepare your body for the practicing astral projection in various ways.

PREPARE FOR TRAVEL – Since it is often easier to reach the needed states of heightened awareness and relaxation in the early hours of the morning, you should begin then to prepare for astral travel. You can also do this at night, in the last moments before you lie down to go to sleep. Astral travel is a purely personal experience, so do what is best for you.

Since you will need to be in a state of complete relaxation, you should prepare while in a place that you feel comfortable. Lie down in your bed and relax your body and your mind. Astral travel is more comfortable to do when alone, so if you regularly sleep with someone else in the room, you might want to sleep in another room while you prepare. A time when you are alone is best so that no one could accidentally walk in and disturb your travels. Get rid of any noise that might distract you, and close the windows and the curtains to allow the room to be dark.

Lie on your back in whichever room you have chosen. Try to clear all distracting thoughts out of your mind as you close your eyes and relax. Your goal here is to attain a state of complete body and mind relaxation. Systematically flex your muscles and then let them rest. Begin with the toes and then work your way up to your head and neck. Make sure that every muscle is completely relaxed before you move on to the next one. Don't allow any tension to gather in your neck and shoulders, and breathe deeply and slowly.

Focus on your deep breathing. Try not to let outside thoughts and worries get into your mind. Also, don't become preoccupied with thoughts of astral travel. Right now, all you need to be concerned with is achieving a state of relaxation. If you have quartz crystals, you can use them to raise your vibrations and help them to move faster. Place the crystal on your forehead over your Third Eye and let your mind clear as you feel the vibrations grow from the crystal. The crystal can also rest on your abdomen or chest or hold it in your hand. It will protect you and empower you because it will give off high vibrations.

Release your soul from your body – Allow your mind and body to get close to sleep but don't fall completely asleep. You need to be in a hypnotic state for astral travel to happen, a place just at the thin line between sleep and awake. Keep your eyes closed and let your thoughts travel to one single part of your body. Focus all of your thoughts on that particular part of your body until you can see it correctly, even with your eyes closed. Let all other ideas fall away while you complete this exercise. Then try to flex that part of your body using only your mind and not your muscles. See your toes wiggling, or your fingers curling into a fist in your mind and keep picturing this until you feel as though these parts are moving. Now broaden the focus of your thoughts to include your entire body. Use only the power of your mind to move your head, arms, and legs. Keep focusing steadily on this technique until you can use just your mind to move your whole body.

Now you will probably feel a series of waves as your soul gets ready to leave your body. If you feel fear, your soul might hesitate, so try not to fear this part. Let the vibrations take over you as your soul prepares to depart on its astral travels. Continue to remain relaxed while you imagine the room that you are lying in. In your mind, move your body so that you can stand up. Once you are standing, look around the space where you are resting. Now keep using the powers of your mind to walk across the room and turn and look at your body lying on the bed. If you can feel that you are looking at yourself from across the room, then the out of body experience is successful. Your body and your conscious self are now separate entities. You might need a lot of practice to get to this point. Anyone can participate in astral travel if they desire and are willing to practice and have faith. If you are having trouble altogether leaving your body, just practice moving an arm or a leg until you have mastered it. And once you are done with your travels, you will return to your body. Let your soul sink back in, and then move your toes and fingers physically to help yourself fully awaken.

Complete your exploration – When you have finally gained the ability to leave your body, you will want to have some confirmation that you are really in two separate worlds at the same time. When you have been able to leave your body, turn to look at yourself, and then return to your body, you will try something different the next time. You will leave your body, but you will not turn around to look at yourself. You will leave the room that your body is lying in, and you will walk to another place in the house. Pick up an object in the other space, maybe an item that you never really paid any attention to in your physical self. Remember as many details of the object as possible, paying attention to its size, shape, and color. Now return to your body and wake yourself up. Get off the bed and walk into the other room and find the object you had before. See if the details are just the way you remember them from your travels.

Once you have mastered astral travel, make more changes on future trips. Try to go to new locations that are less familiar to you. Always make a note of details where you are, and try to remember things that you will verify when you are back in your physical body. After you do this a few times, you will be able to go to places that are unfamiliar to you and then return to those places with your physical body, and they will seem familiar to you. Astral travel is not dangerous. You might feel more secure, picturing a bright white light surrounding you while you travel, a light that will protect you from harm.

Dream Control

If you have ever started dreaming and then suddenly known that you were in a dream, then you had a lucid dream. You were also experiencing a lucid dream if you have taken control of the path that your plan was taking. Usually, when people dream, they have no idea that they are dreaming; they are just doing it. Some people can go into a dream and be completely aware that they are dreaming and in control. Lucid dreams have been recorded since the time of the ancient Greeks.

Like most of the dreams that you have, lucid dreams will happen during those periods of rapid eye movement type of sleep. It usually occurs spontaneously, although some people can train themselves to enter a lucid dream state. The ability of people to influence their dreams has a great deal of variation. Some people will wake up immediately, and some will continue with the dream. Some people can control the entire dream or certain parts of it. Lucid dreaming will allow you to explore the worlds inside your mind while fully aware that you are in a dream. It is an almost magical feeling.

Lucid dreaming may have different applications in the practical world. It can help people to lessen fears or phobias. If someone who has recurring nightmares can become lucid during that nightmare, they may be able to work through their fears. People with phobias can dream about the dread and then use it to control their worries. Therapies like this are possible because the dream state's environment is a safe place that you can quickly leave if the situation becomes too harsh. Lucid dreaming can also be used as entertainment because you can go anywhere you want while you are in the dream state.

There are techniques that you can use if you would like to become better at lucid dreaming. One of these techniques is called reality testing. This test involves a way to verify whether you dream both in the dream and real life. During different times of the day, look at your surroundings, and see how you react. Check your surroundings to see if you are awake or asleep. Set an alarm clock for every two to three hours during the day to make sure you are awake. During a dream, you can look into a mirror to see if you can see yourself. Try to push your hand through your other hand or a wall because you will not be able to if you are awake. See if your hands look familiar to you. Look at the clock on the wall. If you are awake, the time will seem to crawl. If you are in a dream, then the time will continuously change and fluctuate. Pinch your nose and see if you can still breathe.

Try to write down your dreams in a journal every morning as soon as you wake up. When you take the time to write down your dreams, you will be forced to recall the details, which can help you know more about your dream. It can also help you plan a particular dream for lucid dreaming because it is easier to take control when it is something you like or a familiar subject you dream about.

You might sometimes feel that you are trapped in a lucid dream with no way to escape, but there are methods for waking yourself up. If you yell while dreaming, it is a signal for your brain to wake up. Open your eyes and blink rapidly. Try to activate a different part of your mind by reading something in your dream. And if all else fails, go to sleep in your vision because this will disrupt the dream sequence.

CHAPTER 8
Spiritual Beings And The Third Eye

Having a Third Eye that is open and fully functional will enable you to see the entities that come from other astral planes and reside with you on Earth. The ability to see these beings depends on you being in tune with your psychic abilities. You will meet beings familiar to you, and some will seem unique. Receiving messages from people who have passed over, advice from your spiritual guides and deceased loved ones, and psychic information from the energy fields of other people is a part of daily life as a modern mystic.

While your physical eye will show you what is in the world around you, your Third Eye will open you to the possibilities in the astral world. While it is essential to have wide-open eyes to see things, a wide-open Third Eye will allow you to see life beyond life. It is a sense that sends and receives information. You will use your Third Eye to answer questions and understand hidden connections with other people. You will feel more powerful and more empathetic as the possibilities open up before you.

Beings currently walk the Earth disguised as humans, deliberately confusing and fooling you. You might never know who you are dealing with when it comes to a spirit. Any spirit you might encounter can be evil and ugly spiritually or kind and loving, but you may not know until you become close to them. The spirit form is invisible to most people, and you will only be able to see them in their human form.

Earthbound Spirits

Instead of going out of your area, as it should when it removes from the body, the nucleus of the spirit stays behind, trapped on earth, and the nucleus generates a spirit of its own. The energy of the spirit gathers to recreate the form of its lost human being, and it takes on the characteristics of a ghost. It will put aside the fact that it was once human and lives as a form of energy attached mostly to a place or object of former importance. Spirits that are bound to earth have no timeline and sense of time. They have no permanent human form, for they have no hunger or thirst. They will drift unattached until a living person comes along to give them someone to attach with.

An unattached spirit will become a ghostly being when it encounters the human it wants to attach with. Those people who are naturally more sensitive will attract more of these spirit entities. Not every soul will go toward the light at the moment of crossing over from life to death. Some passing souls either do not recognize the light, or they are afraid the light might not be genuine. The mind of the spirit may not trust the light. These spirits will cling to the people they know and love on earth, refusing to cross over at the moment of death. A person like you will come along and give the lost spirit a person to attach to, someone to make new adventures with. The entity the spirit attaches to will help the spirit to grow stronger. Your life force can feed the spiritual side of the ghost. Spirits use their force field to gather particles from electromagnetic fields. This enables them to appear to others, using colors, sounds, or aromas that attract the other entity.

Loved ones who have passed on will show themselves to loved ones by entering their immediate realm or appearing through dreams. When this happens, the spirit must invade the realm of reality, which will give off a gold or silver glow. The spirits will also use small creatures like birds or butterflies to appear to their loved ones left behind.

They might also turn the living person's attention to a particular song, create a coincidence, or waft a fragrance; they do something that stirs the memory of the living person. Other times they will activate a specific memory in the mind of the human they are trying to attract. They can even use a form of a hand to caress the skin of their loved ones. This is an act that takes an enormous amount of effort and focus on the part of the spirit. Still, to them, the possibility of making contact with a loved one is worth the effort.

Knowing your Spirit Guide

Everyone has a spirit guide, a being of light, ancestor, angel, or other entity whose one job is to surround you with love, supporting and guiding you on your journey through life. Your guide may have been with you before in another life. It might be a person you once knew or a loving ancestor determined to help you. You will always have a relationship with your guide as they are there to help you, but you have free will when communicating with your spirit guide. They will stand beside you silently, waiting as they cannot make actual contact with you unless you initiate the contact. This rule becomes voided if you find yourself in the middle of a life-threatening emergency. This information is vital for you to remember so that you do not think your spirit guide is not present with you at all times.

Your first step in making contact with your spirit guide is to have faith that they are with you because if you do not believe in them, you will never be able to communicate with them. And you will most likely have more than one spirit guide. Some of your companions have been with you since birth, and some came along when you needed exceptional help. If you need more spirit guides, you can request them to come to you. They will all work together because they have your best interest in mind. Your spirit guide team might include any or all of the following:

Ascended Masters were humans at one time, and many of them return to act as spirit guides. As leaders in the spirit world, as they were in the human world, they are now guiding your spiritual development and keeping you safe in the world.

Helper Angels are freelance angels who wander around searching for a human with a particular need or are in a specific situation where they need assistance.

Departed Loved Ones are those people you have known who have passed on but became your spirit guide. Any human being who has passed on can become a spirit guide, and they usually look for humans with interests similar to theirs or members of their own family. If you are a nurse, your departed loved one might be a former nurse as they will understand your feelings and frustrations.

Guardian Angels belong to you and only you because they have devoted all of their time to taking care of you. They usually come to you before you are born and stay with you until you die. You can reach out to your guardian angel at any time that you need help.

Spirit Animals are animals who have passed on and returned to assist humans on earth. Often, a pet that you once had will return to your life as your spirit animal, although it can be any animal that has something it needs to help you with at that time. They might be teaching lessons related to their living form so that a wolf might teach you about survival, and a fish might assist you with learning to swim.

Archangels are full of powerful energy, and they are the leaders in the world of spirit guides. Those who are sensitive to spirit energy or empathize with you will often feel a surge of power when you call on your archangel. Each of the archangels has one area of specialization.

Your spirit guide can't communicate with you until you communicate with them first, but they can send you little messages when they feel that you need a push in a particular direction. You might see a book on exotic travel on the very day you think you are at the end of your emotional rope. They will also communicate with you by using numbers or sequences of numbers. If your job interview address is a number that you consider to be a lucky number, then that is probably your spirit guide sending you a message. If you hear a song that is especially meaningful to you after a rough day at work, then your spirit guide is sending you a message. They might also send you a dream with an idea to solve a problem you have. There are ways that you can facilitate communication with your spirit guide.

Use some sort of tool for divination. There are many of these tools you can use like runes, tarot cards, and oracle cards. Before you use any of these, hold them in your hand, and ask your spirit guide to assist you. Use thoughts to send your spirit guide a message. You can have an idea or make a formal request or prayer; any communication method will reach your spirit guide. Develop some sort of spiritual practice that you do regularly. You can have a routine that you do daily, weekly, or monthly as long as you have a ritual of your own.

Work to improve your intuition. You will be able to improve your powers of clairvoyance with study and practice. Begin by practicing with small things that are relatively meaningless. You can try to think where a coworker will choose to go for lunch before inviting them out. Or dump a few of an item into a bowl, like mini marshmallows or marbles, and try to guess how many there are before you count them.

Spend some time studying the idea of the spirit guide. If you take the time to know what they are about, you will be easier to communicate with.
Surrender a problem to your spirit guide. If you have a question that you just can't solve, give it to your spirit guide and let them show you the way. Do this even if all you need is a little break from the events of life. Even surrendering the issue for a little while will give you a mental break, and the spirit guides will have an opportunity to send you some ideas.

Assign your spirit guides their name. Give them a name that is one of your favorites or one that is meaningful to you. It is easier to talk with someone when you know their name. This familiarity will make you more likely to connect with them regularly because it will make them seem more real to you. Start a journal to write about your spirit guide. You can also use this journal to write messages to your spirit guide to ask for their guidance and help. You can also keep a list of signs that they send to you. Watch for signs from your spirit guide. As you spend more time watching for alerts, you will be able to see them more often. And as you grow more alert to your spirit guides sending you signs, they will begin to send even more.

Try to be more present in the everyday. You need to be mentally present in your life if you want to know when your spirit guide sends you a message. People often miss notifications because they are too busy hurrying and don't see the message. Engage is a period of quiet reflection daily, even if it is only thirty minutes. Meditation is a proven method for clearing accumulated thoughts from your mind.

Earth Angel

Angels on earth are real heavenly angels who have been born into a human body so that they can carry out essential missions here on earth. Earth angels are here to open the hearts of others and show them the goodness of true love. They will work to protect people from further harming one another and to preserve the environment. They also want to raise the vibrancy of earth and humanity to communicate with each other and the spirit world more accessible

Earth angels are highly sensitive people who cannot tolerate any form of violence. Being guided by the Laws of the Universe that pertain to trust, purity, and love, they automatically expect that all people will feel the same way, which is why their hearts are often broken and their spirits crushed by the evils of the world. They do not remain sad for long, even though they will never understand the world's violent ways.

They will often look much younger than they are because their happy outlook on life keeps them young at heart. As children, they were frequently bullied or teased because of their different behavior and appearance. Earth angels are highly sensitive to changes in the earth's energy and the people around them. They see all people as good people, even with the shortcomings and imperfections that the Earth angels look past. People often take advantage of their excellent nature because of their kindness, which is often mistaken for weakness. But the Earth angel sees misfortune as a blessing in disguise because they are eternal optimists and never stop believing in people's good.

Many Earth Angels have a difficult childhood. They are often misunderstood by their family members and made to feel that their kindness and gentleness make them look weak. Thus, many Earth angels think that they do not fit in and do not belong here on earth. They may spend time staring up into the night sky and hoping to go home as soon as possible. All of the negative experiences they have might give them low self-esteem. They continuously apologize for things that are not their fault because they feel guilty about everything.

But even with all of the negativity in their lives, Earth angels have tremendous patience and are eternal optimists. They will stay in a relationship that most people would have given up on. The Earth angel needs to reach a total breaking point before they abandon anyone. They always have kind words and words of wisdom for everyone, which is good because everyone brings their problems directly to the Earth angel. They will ignore their own needs in favor of taking care of the needs of the world. But do not take the Earth angel out into a crowded place. They will not do well there because of all of the chaos and noise. Earth angels like solitude and peace.

Earth angles see peace, beauty, and love abundantly in nature. They view the world with awe and astonishment because the world is a beautiful place full of beauty. They are protective of the planet and nature. And no matter what form a life takes, the Earth angel will love everyone equally. They feel interconnected with the Universe and the world, a great oneness with everything and everyone. And no matter how old the Earth angel is, they will still believe in fairy tales and miracles. They have no fear of death because, for them, it means they are going home.

Divination

Many of the cultures around the world practice the same divinatory arts but call them by different names. Divination is the ability to predict, foretell, or foresee or receive inspiration from a god. It attempts to achieve insight into a situation or question by using rituals or processes related to the occult or standard practice. The diviner will either make contact with some supernatural or spiritual agency or read omens, events, or signs. It can be viewed as a method to systematically organize the random and disjointed facts of existence so that they can be used to provide insight into a current problem.

In ancient Greece, both seers and oracles used the art of divination. A prophet is a person who provides prophetic precognition or prediction or insightful counsel regarding the future, using information that was supplied by data received from gods. The prophecies the oracles provided were considered to be the words that came directly from the gods. Of greater importance for the primary source of divination were the seers, since more of them were available. Seers did not speak directly to the gods, as oracles did. They interpreted signs that the gods provided. Seers used any method at their disposal to divine the word of the gods. The oracles' advantage over the seers was that the prophets could fully answer a question where a seer could only respond with yes or no answers.

Man has long had a passion for knowing their destiny, which led to divination. Divination provides answers for current events based on what happened in the past and what might happen in the future. There are countless channels for manifesting the intuition that is needed for divination.

Typing the personality of a person has been a prevalent practice in the East for centuries. Especially in Japan, revealing information about an individual's personality will give information on the person's inhibiting and productive traits, destiny, possible future parenting techniques, and compatibility regarding marriage. They often consider a person's personality as the driving factor when it comes to deciding compatibility for relationships. The Chinese swear by the Chinese zodiac signs based on the birth year of the individual matching with a particular animal. They often mix in traits of celestial types, as are found in the planets. In the East, they also have a divine personality using yin and yang, the four essential elements, and the cardinal directions. Numerology uses a different number based on numbers that are significant in a person's life, such as their date of birth or the letters in their names. Divination is accomplished with many different methods depending on the religion and the items they have available at their disposal.

TEA READING – Reading the leftover tea leaves or coffee grounds at the bottom of a cup is a complex form of divination and gives the reader numerous and different ways. The idea is to see an image and ascertain its meaning.

TAROT – While it is not known who created the first deck of Tarot cards, it is known that this is the most popular divination method, and it has been in use for centuries. Beyond their use for divination, Tarot cards are also used to connect current events and all possible connections. There are infinite combinations, and one or more will have the ability to solve all problems.

GRAINS OF CORN – Early civilizations in North and South America regularly used divination to gather knowledge. They linked the practice with the sciences of meteorology and astronomy. They were especially interested in determining when to plant certain crops and mark the calendar seasons. A unique method of divination was to use grains of corn. These corn grains are thrown onto a white cloth or a flat surface, and then the answer is determined based on the way the grains fell.

SCRYING – This is one of the oldest divination methods, and it was practiced by many of the ancient cultures. In ancient Mesopotamia, they used oil that was poured into unique bowls. The ancient Greeks looked into the reflection on metals and in mirrors. Scrying was practiced in ancient Egypt using ink. The Aztecs read thoughts in obsidian. The idea is to look into the reflection for answers to questions and desired knowledge. This ancient practice eventually led to crystal readings and the powers associated with gazing into the crystal ball.

SAND DIVINATION – Reading the shapes in the sand is one of the oldest and most beautiful forms of divination. Messages found in the sand layers were read, and this method was frequently used in ancient Muslim communities. The sand can be thrown out on a cloth or a board specially made for sand divination, and it is necessary to know the codes that the geometric figures correspond to.

Precognition and Spirituality

Precognition is the ability to know that things are going to happen before they even occur. Since ancient people's times, precognition has been associated with dream states and trances that involve such phenomena as premonitions, second sight, fortune-telling, and prophecy. Events of foreknowledge usually happen when a person receives a mental scenario in short sequences. Precognition can occur when you are awake or asleep.

You can seek answers in many different methods for your spiritual questions. If you are open enough, you will receive dialog directly from channeling that can be impactful and inspirational. Opening your heart and soul to the higher vibrations from sources outside of ordinary teachings will leave you wide open to receive the images known as precognition.

The knowledge that you seek is already inside of you, but it needs to be unlocked to enable you to have access to the information. You can remove resistance to your spiritual awareness no matter where you arrived from or where you currently are in your spiritual past. If you think you do not possess this ability if you doubt your capabilities, which are just negative information from you that seeks answers for your emotional and spiritual problems.

Precognition is part of clairvoyance. Too many people do not want to use their Third Eye or see into the future. They may fear the unknown or what they might see during their spiritual journey. If you're going to see clearly, you will need to be able to accept things that could not make any sense at that time, and you need to be able to take them without question because many of these truths will be far beyond the realm of what is believed to be possible.

Real precognition lies in collecting the details of the image you see. Anyone can see a future vision, but taking note of the elements is an integral part of the view. Precognition will provide you with a depth of understanding you never had before.

Etheric Entities on the Physical Plane

Magic and spiritual work often involve the ability to work with entities of the etheric. An etheric entity is a being that is energetic and non-material. Everyone is a multi-dimensional creature with multiple forms of their body on many different densities and activity levels. The only vehicle capable of moving through an incarnation is the physical body. Then the physical form branches out into multiple energies and fields known as the plasma body, the dream body, the astral body, the meridian body, the auric body, and the energy body. You cannot see the other planes of existence and densities' light resonant frequencies, although you can feel them. You are only able to see the physical plane of yourself.

When you begin your awakening process, you will realize that the world is basically upside down and backward from what it should be. Your new awareness will give you the need for information that will lead you to the darkness of the world and out into the light on the other side. As you search, you will encounter the entities of the etheric. These entities will vary significantly in their sentience, power, and form. Those who possess a greater complexity of etheric patterns will have greater sentience. Their influence on the etheric level is directly related to their energy levels.

You might be allowed to interact with several different forms of etheric entities. There will be deities, disembodied humans, complex spirits, cultivated spirits, and simple spirits. All of these entities are the different aspects of the multifaceted cosmos. The gods are the broader fields of power and consciousness within the etheric realm. Humans most often see them because they possess the ability to manifest themselves to humans in ways in which they can be seen. The various spirits are smaller and more localized entities within the etheric realm. They can change their form as they please. You will draw upon a larger collective of consciousness by interacting with these entities.

You will need to develop the skills required to see and communicate with them to work effectively with these entities. You will use etheric perception to become aware of their presence and etheric communication to interact with them. The type of interaction you have will depend on the nature of your goal, the relationship between you and the entity, and the type of entity you are interacting with. The reality of the etheric and the entities is entirely subject to the interpretation of your mind

CHAPTER 9
Life After Life

Man has long been fascinated by the gateway to the universe that runs through the Third Eye. Your soul will connect directly to this gateway and bring the energy of the universe to your life. Your brain and all of its components direct everything in your bodies. Your soul shines a light on the Third Eye, where the energy of the body and the mind meet as one. Pictures of saints and other holy figures show them with a golden halo of light surrounding their heads because they were aware of the goodness of their souls. Their attention was focused on their souls and the radiance that comes from the Third Eye. They operated out of that awareness that the soul was one with the mind. They achieved the climb to the peak of the sensory pyramid. Even those people who were not clairvoyant appeared with rings of radiance surrounding their heads.

Mediation allows the person who is meditating to spend time focusing on their soul. It is a process to withdraw from the body's sensations and the mind, the thought apparatus. Those who are experienced at focusing their attention on meditation can expand their focus to greater heights. They can knock on the door of heaven. Their soul will withdraw away from their body as it passes through the process of removing itself from the body. While the mind and the self are still in focus at this time, the feeling is in your emotional and spiritual body.

Elevated Souls on Earth

The advanced souls on earth have a difficult spiritual journey ahead of them. Because of the hardships they suffer, they want to spread healing and love around the world. As children, they often had no one to help them, so they wanted to help everyone. The trauma and turmoil that they suffered as children have made them into loving and giving souls.

Their job on earth is to restore humanity to a way of balance, love, and harmony. They want to alleviate the chaos in the world and restore order. They are on a spiritual path designed to make life better for themselves and the world around them. They are connected to the world in a profoundly selfless manner. They relate deeply to the entities in the world, plants, animals, and people. No matter how crazy their journeys might be, they are always peaceful and at peace.

Instead of being full of bitterness, they are still seeking a higher purpose in life. They like to spend their time helping and teaching others as they encourage self-love.

Advanced souls spend their lives trying to bring out the best in other people. They shine their lights brightly so that those in need will know who to come to for assistance. They emanate charisma and charm, and their magnetic field guides people to them. They heal hearts and souls and share their wisdom with anyone who will listen. They bring positive change to the world with their goodness and love.

Daydreams for Life

Daydreaming is the constant stream of consciousness that detaches people from their current external tasks. It directs their attention away from external items and leads them to internal and personal matters. This redirection is a common phenomenon that is almost everyone's daily lives. The various other names for daydreaming are random thoughts, fantasy, and mind wandering. Some daydreams are beneficial, and some are disruptive, and no two imaginations are identical. There are five potential positive functions that daydreaming serves: relief from boredom, dishabituation, attention cycling, creative thinking, and future thinking.

A distinct and very adaptive function of daydreaming is the relief from boredom. Daydreaming allows people to let their thoughts wander while they are doing repetitive or monotonous tasks. This wandering will not cause the external activity to be disrupted, but it will temporarily detach the person. Daydreaming does seem to make time pass better. Dishabituation is needed when the external stimulus is continuously repeated and causes a decrease in internal stimulation. This boredom happens when learning is repetitive. People learn more effectively when that learning is broken up into parts instead of given all at once. The ability to daydream lets you relieve the strain on your mind caused by intense, repetitive learning by mentally stepping away for a while, and you can return when you choose to.

An adaptive function of daydreaming is attention cycling. It helps to keep your behaviors in optimal condition when you face multiple problems at the same time. This cycling will let you choose the appropriate action for the situation when you are dealing with various situations. Daydreaming will let you switch between different thoughts and streams of information when you have many goals. Creative thinking associates daydreaming with increased creativity. If you spend some time daydreaming while trying to solve a complicated problem, you will find your most productive moments come when you are daydreaming. Intentional daydreaming is constructive when it is used in periods of intense thought.

Future thinking is also known as autobiographical thinking, which gives you the ability to anticipate and speculate about future events. It allows for better planning and the opportunity to prepare for future events and goals. It can also help keep you mind off your relevant goals while deciding on the best course of events to help you reach that goal.

Scientists and psychologists have been interested in the wanderings of the mind for years. They know that the brain has specific structures known as the default network of the brain. This network links several areas of the brain together that are involved in sensory experiences. The technical term for these impulses in the brain is the independent thoughts of the brain's stimulus. They cause the brain to think about something apart from the events coming in from outside sources. In everyday speech, the wanderings of the mind are also known as daydreams and fantasies.

Besides serving to entertain you when you are bored, daydreams serve useful purposes. They will help you to explore your inner experiences and ideas. People specifically engage their internal stimulus systems when trying to make moral or ethical decisions, understand what other people are thinking, imagine an event that might occur in the future, and contemplate their own past experiences.

It is your default network that makes your daydreaming possible. The nature of your daydreams will have a direct effect on your mind and soul. Men will dream more often when their lives are unsatisfactory. Women don't desire more often due to lower satisfaction with life, but their daydreams will become more vivid. Both men and women who daydream about friends and family members generally report being more satisfied with their lives. People who are not happy with their lives will often daydream about fictional characters or people from their past, especially in romantic situations. People who daydream like this tend to have less social support than most people and are often lonely. There are four practical ways in which you can use your daydreaming to your advantage.

- Do not allow your daydreams to interfere with what you need to do, but don't let them interfere with your creativity. You need to daydream now and then feed your imagination, but not so much that your daydreaming interferes with what you need to get done in your daily life. Make sure you are paying enough attention to experience to get done what you need to get done.
- When you need to focus, you will need to turn off your brain's default network actively. When you deactivate the system, you will have your best chance to learn new concepts and skills. So if your daydreams are getting in the way of your daily life tasks, then feel free to turn down the network's volume.
- Change your daydreams if they are not satisfying to you. Try to fantasize about the relationships that you are currently in and ways to make them better. Daydreaming about relationships that you will never have will make you more dissatisfied with your current life situation.
- Your memory can be helped or hurt by your tendency to daydream. When your daydreams keep you closer to home, your daily performance will be better than it will if your fantasies take you to places that are far away.

Daydreams are often used to reveal aspects of the personal life of an individual. Based on the details you imagine during a daydreaming episode, you will be informed about your personality. When you rehearse or replay your thoughts or actions in your mind, this is known as self-reflecting daydreaming. This form of trance can have results that are both detrimental and beneficial. You will suffer from an increase in negative thoughts if you focus too much on negative reviews from the past or imagining negative possibilities in the future. Use self-reflective daydreaming for positive imaginings, such as ways to show creativity or planning for the future. It can be beneficial for you and result in more positive thoughts.

People who are stuck in boring jobs or are unemployed are more likely to daydream than people who have exciting or at least satisfying jobs. Much like nighttime dreaming, daydreaming is when your mind will consolidate all of the information received on a specific topic or event. Brain areas that are associated with solving complex problems are highly active when people are daydreaming. So regular daydreaming might help you to achieve success in your life as you sort through your issues.

Dreaming and Symbolism

Dreams are thought to be messages from higher powers or the world of spirits. Plans often contain images and symbols that have a particular meaning in the natural world. The number of symbols or images that come to people in their dreams is countless. Suppose you can dream about something that something can carry a deeper emotional and psychological significance than just the image of the item brings. One typical image that appears in dreams is the image of a house. Different people will read other things into the appearance of a home in their goals. It might be a place they once lived, it relates to the physical body of the person, or it might hold deeper meaning if it represents something from your childhood. A house is a physical representation of your emotional and spiritual self. If you dream about a place you lived in as a child, you might be looking for a simpler and happier life. If you dream about exploring a strange house, you may be seeking change in your life. If one of the house rooms is not accessible, that might represent something in your life that you are not yet ready to examine. The way you react to the house and what you do in the dream is the key to understanding its meaning in your physical life. There is no single meaning for images and symbols seen in dreams, but some pictures of plans are so common that they carry a generally accepted definition.

- Being chased in a dream does not indicate the actual chase, but what you are running away from, which represents something you are avoiding in your life or great fear.
- Food symbolizes nourishment, knowledge, or energy and is directly related to your spirituality, emotions, and intellect. It might also mean that you are hungry for new knowledge or insights in your life.
- Dreams of water are tied to your current emotional state.
- If you dream about a baby, it doesn't necessarily mean that you want one, unless you do. Dreaming about a baby represents the desire for personal growth or professional development.
- Dreams about vehicles of any kind often reflect the direction that you think your life is going in or an obstacle that you need to face.
- Dreaming about being nude in a place where no one else is nude usually means that you feel vulnerable or fear psychological or emotional exposure.
- If you dream about different people, it reflects the various aspects of your personality.

- Death doesn't always need to be a negative omen because it means that you need to drastically change something in your life in the world of dreams.
- Falling can be the ominous sign that you need to let go of something in your life. But it can also be a serene feeling, especially if you know you need to let go of that thing.
- Adults who dream of being in the classroom are often looking for inspiration in lessons they learned in childhood.
- You might feel that you lack control over your personal life if you dream about being paralyzed.
- When you fly in your dreams, it relates to the control you feel you have over your own life, and whether you fly well or poorly correlates to your perceived level of control. Flying high indicates that you are confident and euphoric; flying low means you are frustrated or depressed.

Awareness of the Aura

Reading an aura is like looking into someone's soul because the ambiance is created from the colors that correspond to the energy that comes from the person. The atmosphere is the magnetic field of life that surrounds all living people. Every aura comprises seven layers that form one aural body, the subtle inner body's outer reflection. More energy means a more massive atmosphere, so people who have suffered in life will generally have larger auras than young or have lived a sheltered life. Clairvoyants can read the auras of people and the scenes, blockages, and energy patterns in the aura. Every color has its meaning.

The aura is made of seven bodies of energy and three planes. The spiritual plane is your connection to the divine and your intuition. The astral plane is the bridge between your spiritual plane and your physical plane and comes from the link to your heart. And the physical plane includes your mental body, emotional body, and your etheric body. The colors of your aura directly correspond to the chakras in your body. If any of the chakras are imbalanced, that will reflect on how their color displays in the aura. This reflection will tell how the person is feeling spiritually, emotionally, mentally, and physically. The aura will continuously change colors and depth of color to mirror the chakras in the person. The energy fields will attach to the person with little attachment cords. There might also be tears in the aura if different chakras are severely damaged.

The colors that are found in the aura that directly relate to the chakra are these:

- White – peace and truth – The Crown Chakra
- Purple or Indigo – wisdom and divinity – The Third Eye Chakra
- Blue or indigo – self-expression and communication – The Throat Chakra
- Green – love and nurturing – The Heart Chakra
- Yellow – intellect and self-esteem – The Solar Plexus Chakra
- Orange – ambition, and creativity – The Sacral Chakra
- Red – passion, and vitality – The Root Chakra

To perceive and accurately interpret an aura, you need to be aware of yourself enough to know the place where you end and the other person begins. If they are not, then the reading may only reflect themselves and not their perception of the other person. Spirit mediums are easily able to read auras. Reading a person's aura can help determine chakra blockages and imbalances, precognition, and determining strengths of personality and spirit.

Seeing into the Afterlife

After you leave your physical body, your identity, your stream of consciousness, will continue to reside in the astral plane. This entity might be your soul or your spirit, or even some part of your essential role. The destination that your essence takes after your death will depend on what your beliefs are in the physical plane. You may move on to take up residence for eternity in Heaven. You might be reborn into the world and begin life again with no actual memory of the experience you had before.

Everyone will die eventually. Many people fear death because there is no way to know what is beyond death in the afterlife. People have near-death experiences and describe beautiful colors, softness, and the bright light at the end of the tunnel, but that might be nothing more than the corridor that houses the end of life; it might have nothing at all to do with experience in the next world. It is assumed to be a glimpse of Heaven, but no one knows for sure.

Atheists have varying views on the afterlife. Heaven is not a viable destination for them since they do not believe in God. However, some think that there is some possibility for reincarnation or life on an astral plane. Buddhists believe in reincarnation but not in the soul. They teach that the deceased only wait a short time in a state of suspension before taking on their new form. Hindus also believe in reincarnation, and they even concede to the presence of the soul. Christian ideals depend on the denomination, but there is an abiding feeling in God and Heaven's existence as a destination for the soul after death occurs.

So the presence or absence of any form of afterlife, and what might happen there, will depend solely on what you believe will happen there when you die.

The Ascended Masters are spiritually enlightened and have moved beyond all of their incarnations in the physical realm. They have taken the Fifth Initiation and can dwell in the Fifth Dimension's heavenly kingdom. They were known as Spiritual Master, Shaman, Commoner, Guru, Yogi, or Master. When the Master is able, he will gain full union with the Mighty Presence.

As individuals on earth, the Masters learned all of the lessons of life during their incarnations. They were able to fulfill their divine plan, balance out at least fifty-one percent of their negative karma with positive karma, and gained the necessary mastery over the physical plane's limitations. In this understanding, the Ascended Master has achieved a state where he is very much like a god. His ascension has reunited him with himself in the image of the gods.

The Ascended Masters act as teachers for humanity, working from the spirit realm. They do to attend to humanity's need for spiritual assistance, and they act to motivate and inspire the spiritual growth of the individual. Anyone who wishes to achieve the rank of Ascended Master has the power to do so if they will only follow the path that begins on earth and continues through their reincarnations until they have fulfilled all of the requirements.

Reincarnation

Also known as transmigration or rebirth, reincarnation is the religious or philosophical view that the soul or spirit will begin a new life in a new form after their physical body dies. Many of the Indian religions, like Hinduism, Sikhism, Buddhism, and Jainism, teach the belief in reincarnation.

When you leave your present body and are reincarnated into a new life form, the idea is that you will strive to live better than you did in your previous life. The structure of your reincarnation will depend on how you lived in your last experience. Those who lived poorly or misbehaved will be reincarnated as something undesirable, something like a bug or a poisonous plant. Those who lived a good life would return as something more pleasant. The next life's quality in any particular incarnation will depend on the person's karma as they move through images. Someone with more negative karma than positive karma will need to continue reincarnating until rebalancing their karmic bank. This rebalancing is not used as a type of punishment but as a method of teaching. If someone's karmic balance is more negative than positive, they have not learned to let go of their ego and live righteous lives.

When a person finally learns to live the most moral incantation, they will find salvation after death. This liberation is the actual pursuit of reincarnation. Most Western ideas picture reincarnation as the desire to go back to a better life than the person will truly enjoy, but that is not true. The goal of reincarnation is to stop being reborn so that the soul will know eternal peace.

People in the west are experiencing a developing interest in reincarnation. As the ancient world's teachings become better known, people seek new answers to the world's current problems. They become more accepting of the old ideals and teachings, one of which is reincarnation. They have hundreds of years of beliefs to go through while deciding if reincarnation will be part of their new belief system. This desire to believe in life after life reinforces man's desire to find meaning and purpose in their present lives. It is difficult to accept that one day all of this will be over and we will be gone. But if we are reincarnated, we will have the chance to return to earth and do the things we couldn't do before or make amends for past wrongs. This desire gives us the motivation and vision to explore who we really are and strive to achieve the best part of yourself that you can. In doing this, we will assure ourselves the best possible life when we do return to earth in our new form to live life on earth again.

CHAPTER 10
Improved Life With An Open Third Eye

The intuition of your Third Eye binds your conscious mind with your spiritual mind. It is the spiritual you that is aware of your emotions and your experiences. Your Third Eye is a magnificent tool that brings you to deep understanding and insight. Once your Third Eye is opened, you will begin to evolve into your potential of the highest growth. Your intuition will grow strong after the Third Eye is opened, and it will be evident to you in many different situations.

People whose Third Eye chakras are open have easy access to their intuition. Whether they've reached illumination or are still moving toward it, these people have a deeper understanding of reality and the nature of the human condition. They tend to be unflappable and feel good to be around because of their relaxed personality. It isn't that they don't care. They see things from a broader perspective (the bigger picture) and understand that everything is unfolding the way it needs to; they know through personal experience that all in existence is connected. We are all extensions of divine source energy. These people don't worry because they know that all will work out for the greater good, which is true enough.

Your Third Eye has been inside your physical body since birth, waiting to connect to your spiritual self. It has always been activated and spinning. It was active in your early childhood when you had confidence and will-power, and you trusted in the truth of everyone and everything. In childhood, you were powered by life and all the dreams you had for the future. You were likely sensitive to the happenings around you, and you frequently saw entities that the adults in your life could not see. But you knew they existed, in the days before you became conditioned and no longer believed in the other world.

Developing your Third Eye will once again open the doorway to your psychic reality. It will give you the abilities you left behind in your childhood, your clairvoyance, your projection into the astral plane, and your lucid dreaming. When the Third Eye connection is cultivated, you will no longer be separated from your spirit. Metaphysical connections to the Third Eye will allow you to awaken while in the dream state and pass humanity's normal limits by walking between the realities you perceive.

Negativity comes from a blocked Third Eye, the kind of negativity that brings negative thoughts along with confusion and uncertainty. The highest source of ethereal energy comes from an open Third Eye. Your physical eyes will only see the physical world. The vision from the Third Eye connects the physical world with the spirit world. Gaining access to your Third Eye and all of its powers will give your insight and intuition as well as clarity of mind that will bring powers of concentration and decisiveness. Your Third Eye links you to enhanced imagination, astral projection, lucid dreaming and quality of sleep, and the ability to view others' aura. You will encounter visions and messages of guidance once you open your Third Eye. Use your strength and follow through on what is offered by your intuition, and the strength of your Third Eye will deepen and develop.

It is normal for humans to reach early adulthood carrying with them the fears of the future that bring anxiety and depression. Once the awareness of the spiritual world closes, at about age six, humans become mired in the illusion of their own ego and the pursuit of materialism. Your systems of belief and education will be destroyed when you open your Third Eye. Truth and enlightenment will come to you when you throw off the restraints of old beliefs and ideals. This will prove to be the hardest obstacle to your awakening because you will need to leave all of your old systems of comfort to gain the truth that is waiting for you. When you release that fear of what will happen to you and who you will become, you will then ease into the fields of contentment and compassion that your intuition is always guiding you towards.

In the beginning, your ego will reject the discipline and focus that you are trying to teach yourself. Your ego will go to great lengths to distract you since it needs to keep you away from the picture of the perfect world that you are attempting to grow toward. It is through the process of surrender to the wisdom of your Third Eye that your life will unfold. That will allow you to gain the greater truth of reality. You will then know that all is well as you bask in your new feelings of self-assuredness.

Your new sense of knowing and understanding will lead you down your new path in life. Even during tough times in your life, you will know what to do and how to proceed. The truth will grow in your mind and heart as you begin to view life more clearly. The illusions of the ego will no longer hold you back. Your childhood abilities will return to aid you in your adult life.

When you open your Third Eye, you enter a massive field of energy. You will access higher planes of consciousness and different astral planes as you realize you are no longer chained by your body and your mind. The new knowledge that love, joy, and peace come from within will surprise and delight you.

Learning to use the field of energy is one of the fun effects of opening your Third Eye. The subtle areas of energy that your physical eyes can't see will be apparent in your intuitive center. This field of life is fueled by your thoughts, intentions, and emotions. All living creatures have their own field of vibration. You will realize the connection between your energy field and the energy emitted by other beings and entities.

You will realize you are not just your body, mind, and emotions, and this more profound realization is called inner knowing. Deep meditation will help you arrive at this state. Your intuition will bring you to this realization. You are not just a product of the components of your physical body, feelings, or thoughts, and you are far above the influence of material things. Your intuitive senses prove that you are aware of yourself, experienced, and witness of experiences. You will witness your emotions, thoughts, and spiritual and physical sensations. You will become one with your experiences with this awareness of your attention.

You will access higher planes of consciousness and know ascended masters, deities, guardian angels, spirit guides, Buddha, Jesus. Every ascended master becomes directly accessible to those on earth. The world of the ascended spirits and the astral planes' universal wisdom is yours when your intuition opens. When used with the simple intention, you can connect with these guides and helpers to assist you on your path. Whether that is through divination or receiving healing and support, they will help you along your way.

You will learn that joy, love, and peace are not found outside of you. Most people seek these spiritual pleasures from the attention of other people. These are temporary springs your intuition will guide you away from. You will learn that everything you need will be found inside of you. You will leave behind the constant pursuit of earthly desires that make you suffer from your wanting and searching. You will learn to seek the bottomless well of calm and peace found within you.

You will surrender to the depth within you. Your intuitive awakening will benefit you immediately in beautiful ways after opening your Third Eye. You will have the power to access parts of yourself that might once have been hidden from you.

Your fear of the unknown might haunt you while opening your Third Eye, but this fear will fade as you grow stronger in your energies. As your thoughts direct your energy, if you feel fear, you will create a negative experience during your awakening because of that fear. You will gain access to the depths of love within your own love and enjoy the experience of the awakening. Your mind and heart will determine the speed of your awakening. The more you trust your personal decision and surrender your ego, the more powerfully you will connect.

With your increased intuition and clairvoyant and telepathic abilities, you will desire a more meaningful life. You will need to create an experience more connected to your higher purpose. All souls begin life on earth with their divine mission preprogrammed inside. With your open Third Eye, you will face your true calling and seek your divine mission. Everything new inside you will prompt you to make needed changes. You will seek more meaningful relationships, and you will devote more of your time to pursuits that are meaningful for you. You will seek jobs and activities that will allow you to make a change in the world. You will experience the exalted freedom that comes with eternal love for yourself.

CONCLUSION

Thank you for coming to the end of *Open Your Third Eye*. Let's hope this book was interesting and informative and able to give you all of the tools you will need to achieve all of your goals, no matter what they may be.

The next step is to open your Third Eye and begin your journey to the path of enlightenment and self-realization. Your Third Eye is your doorway to the world beyond the physical world that your physical eyes see. Third Eye vision will put you in touch with all of the powers of the universe and all of the images that were locked to you before. You will have access to astral planes and other worlds. Beings that inhabit these planes will come to you in a fantastic display of connection and awareness.

The beings that will come to you have always been with you, but your open Third Eye will give you greater access to them. You will experience elevated states of consciousness that will increase your psychic abilities and your spirituality. You will learn methods for emptying your mind and truly relax with the power of meditation that enables freedom for your mind.

The power of mysticism will now be open to you. With that will come an ability to develop your automatic writing and extrasensory perception. You may find a new career as a medium, channeling the departed thoughts into forms that are easy for those left behind to comprehend. An open Third Eye will cause you to desire life more accessible to others, with ways in which you can assist others. This channeling might be your new calling in life.

You will also develop control over your dreams, allowing you to indulge in out of body experiences with people from other astral planes. Through the powers of divination, you will enable your powers of precognition. You will also find communications with beings who have gone before so that you can better understand the life beyond life known as reincarnation.

Finally, if you found this book was useful to you in any way, a review on Amazon is always appreciated!

Kundalini

Expand Mind Power, Gain Spiritual Awareness, Open Your Third Eye, Enhance Psychic Abilities and Discover Transcendence

Lisa Blake

INTRODUCTION

Welcome to *Kundalini*. You are about to tap into a significant wealth of knowledge that will allow you to tap fully into the power of your mind.

Each one of us has unlimited potential stored within the very power of our minds. This power enables us to achieve everything from basic day-to-day living to accomplishing extravagant, impressive, and life-changing goals that move us from the ordinary to the extraordinary. While every one of us can tap into this unlimited mind power, very few ever will. Some believe they are not lucky enough to have it, others believe it takes too much work, and others still are not convinced that mind power is real. You are not one of the many who will succumb to these weak thoughts, though. You are one of the strong ones, one of the ones who will take the necessary action to expand your mind power to achieve incredible things in life.

To help you tap into your unlimited potential in a comfortable, step-by-step way, I have defined everything you require to expand your mind power. From understanding what mind power is and where it resides to taking physical, mental, and emotional care of your mind, you will uncover every step required to help you reach your fullest potential. Believe it or not, it is not nearly as challenging as many make it out to be.

The most complicated part of activating your mind power is the element of consistency. Without consistency, nothing will ever stick. You must be willing to rise every day and take action on fueling your mind power if you desire to release yourself from the chains of mediocrity and create success in your life.

With adequate consistency, a hunger for change, and a willingness to do whatever it takes, you will discover there is nothing you cannot do in your life. If you are ready to expand your mind power and awaken the unlimited potential you already have within you, it is time to begin...

CHAPTER 1
What Is Mind Power?

Of all the powers you possess, mind power might be the most significant. Mindpower exists as the root power of everything you accomplish, become, and experience. Anytime you achieve anything in your life, regardless of how easy or complex it may have been to get there, you can be confident that you have tapped into mind power to get you there.

In Kundalini, mind power is achieved by awakening your energies and embodying them as profoundly as possible. The greater your mind power, the closer you are to enlightenment. People will spend their entire lives discovering how they can expand their mind power even further to achieve greater awakening levels.

Many people falsely believe mind power is inherent and that there is nothing you can do to expand or increase your mind power. These are the same people who believe that you achieve results through luck, and more often than not, they are not the "lucky type." Based on what Kundalini teaches, mind power can increase, strengthen, and be used to your advantage in many different ways. Whether you want to expand your business skills, increase your happiness, create better health, or design your dream lifestyle, all of this is achieved through mind power. Still, you might be wondering, what *is* mind power, exactly?

The Kundalini Take on Mind Power

To expand mind power, or to expand consciousness, is the ultimate goal of one's life. There are many practical and spiritual ways that you can identify and work with the energy of mind power, ranging from using your logical and rational brain in earthly matters to engaging in Kundalini yoga and meditation. Often, practitioners will adjust their entire lives to expand into their consciousness's depths. It is said that your mind power will continue to increase to the point that you achieve total enlightenment, at which point you have reached "maximum capacity."

Although mind power can drastically transform your physical life, many claim that the physical benefits of expanding your mind power no longer matter once you reach a significant point of expansion. While people who have experienced lower levels of enlightenment may believe that physical gains are the most remarkable thing about life, those who have experienced higher enlightenment levels are aware that material improvements are less enjoyable. The real enjoyment comes from the power you gain within yourself, and everything you can accomplish with that power, which is far beyond the physical world's fundamental limitations. Whether you want to bring the nonphysical into the material, invent something new, or experience the entirety of who you are, tapping into your unlimited mind power is a phenomenal way to do so.

The Power of Your Thoughts

To invent the light bulb, Thomas Edison first had to think about the value of harnessing the power of light. To develop the telephone, Alexander Graham Bell first had to think about the importance of communicating from great distances. To design the airplane, the Wright brothers first had to think about the importance of traveling through the air. Anytime something has been created or conceived in this world, whether it be magnificent or straightforward, it had first to be thought about, then it could be made. Without first bringing something into our awareness on a thought-level, there is no way to get into our realities on a physical level.

The impressive thing about thoughts is that, once you can think it, you can create it. Our minds are magnificently intelligent, and we possess an incredible capacity to turn any thought into our reality. Even if you cannot presently *see* how it might become your reality, your mind has everything required to pick apart this "problem" and turn your thoughts into your reality. Your thoughts are *the* most powerful thing you have in your life.

Think about it for a moment:

- The last time you were driving home and a detour on your usual route, you quickly resolved that problem by finding an alternate route home.
- When your boss had a challenge and needed you to resolve it, you rapidly thought about a creative solution to that problem.
- Every time you get home and prepare to make dinner, your mind rapidly solves "what to make?"

- The last time you got in an argument and decided you did not want to fight, your mind found a solution to help bring you peace.
- When you last came across an unexpected bill, your mind rapidly discovered a solution to help you pay for it.
- Every time you enter the grocery store with a mission to shop for everything on your list, your mind helps you do it efficiently.

Your mind is continually working to help you solve everyday problems and broader issues that may require more effort or more extensive solutions to get the results you need. Regardless of how small or large the question is or how long it takes you to find the answer, your mind *always* pulls through. As long as you give yourself enough time to focus and implement possible solutions, you find your way through any challenge you make.

This sheer mind power that gets you through everyday issues and more extensive problems you face in your life is the same mind power that invented everything in our modern world. No matter how significant or insignificant, every piece of technology was created through an individual's mind power that was willing to think of it, solve the problem, and bring it into our modern existence. Mindpower truly is the most significant power any one of us has.

Exercising Your Creative Power

The real fuel behind mind power is your creative power. Before you throw the breaks on this whole process and go, "Woah, woah, woah, I'm not creative at all. You should see my painting efforts. Stickmen look fancy compared to the junk I create!" I want to explain what I mean about creative power and emphasize that we all have creative control. Whether or not you can paint a Bob Ross-style painting or create an incredible mosaic table, you possess creative power within you that you tap into every single day. When you map out the quickest route to work each morning, you are harnessing your creative energy. When you wake up and decide what to make for breakfast, what order to get ready for work in, or how to spend your day off, you harness your creative energy. As you read this book and even envision yourself doing any of these things, you are harnessing your creative power. Every day, you are using your creative energy more than you can imagine, even if you are not using it intentionally, yet!

To make changes in your life, you must apply the power of creative thinking to create a new vision of what you want for yourself, and then you can work toward bringing that into your reality. Remember, you can imagine what you can experience, so as long as you can get it in at a thought level, you can create it in your real life.

The current video you are playing in your mind is one that tells you who you are, what you are capable of, what to think, and what to do in your life. By changing the video, you change your perspective, and you experience something more enjoyable in your life. It may seem strange or even unbelievable that change is this simple, but it is. The more you practice changing the video and witnessing something different in your mind, the more you will find yourself experiencing any transformation you desire in life. You begin to embrace the real power of manifesting, and you rapidly realize that you really *can* attract the life of your dreams, purely through the power of your creative thoughts.

Reality at a Thought-Level

Creating your reality from a thought-level is something you already do, naturally. There is no new skill that you need to discover or learn to harness this power and use it to your advantage. The real learning curve is discovering how you can become aware of this process to create your reality from a thought-level *intentionally*.

When you embrace Kundalini as a reality of life, the awakening you experience can alter your thought-patterns and ultimately shift the way you experience, and create, your truth. At first, you might experience chaos in your existence because of how chaotic and overwhelming Kundalini energy can be. As you find comfort in your awakening, you will discover that the mind power afforded to you by your continued awakening alters the way you experience reality and create yours.

I want you to think about the last time you were afraid of something and let fear win. You may have been afraid of your boss rejecting your request for a raise, people judging you for a choice you made, or you making a mistake with something you care much about. Regardless of the specific circumstances, I can almost guarantee that you spent time leading up to that scary event worrying and imagining your fear. You likely sat there, imagining the thing you were afraid of happening, happening. You visualized everything going wrong, you being rejected, shame or embarrassment growing, the catastrophic results of your failure, and every other possible detail you could. Perhaps you even imagined the conversations you would have or the excuses you would give when everything went wrong, and you inevitably screwed everything up.

When you reached the point where you could engage in the very thing that was making you fearful, things either went one of three ways:

- You chickened out.
- You did it and screwed everything up.
- You did it well enough and then suffered a "fear hangover."

Either way, you made the experience harder than it needed to be and capped your potential in that experience because you believed in the fear more than you believe in yourself.

To create a new reality from a thought-level, you need to harness this power you are already magnificent at and use it to your advantage. Using it effectively, you can stop yourself from chickening out and prevent poor or mediocre results by setting yourself up to reach your unlimited potential. Which by the way, your power is available in every moment, no matter how new you might be to something in your life. You do this by *changing the video*.

Change the video by envisioning something more empowering and giving yourself the chance to believe in *that* instead. Rather than thinking everything will go wrong, you will make a fool of yourself, or people will judge you, consider that everything will go right. Believe that your actions and attitude inspire people and that people have a *good* judgment of you, based on how you showed up. Imagine the things people will say to you to congratulate you on your win and the success speech you will share with people when they ask how you did it. By changing the tape, you uncap your potential.

CHAPTER 2
A Clear Overview Of Physical Mind Power

While your thoughts are where the magic happens, your mind power is not purely based on intangible ideas that you experience within your mind. Your brain's health plays a significant role in your control, as it provides you with the ability to have a healthy, well-functioning sense to provide you with your magnificent results in the first place. There are many ways that you can aid the physical wellness of your brain to improve your mind power, and it is suggested that you follow all of them. The stronger your brain is, the stronger your mind power can be, and the fewer limitations you have when it comes to uncapping your potential and creating your magical results.

Although Kundalini is a form of spiritual energy, it has a tangible impact on your physical body. One way that Kundalini affects your body is through affecting your brain, primarily through the creation of new neural pathways, as you begin perceiving and experiencing life in an entirely new way. It is tremendously helpful to discover how you can integrate Kundalini into your practical day to day life, allowing you to experience the energy in a grounded way. Although the goal is enlightenment, enlightenment is best achieved when you can remain grounded and firmly connected to current reality's physical powers.

Neuroplasticity and Neural Pathways

Thoughts are a seemingly magical experience that activates different parts of the brain and then disappears. Each opinion does not necessarily affect your mind, but thinking the same ideas over and over again can completely change your mind. The changes occur through what is known as neuroplasticity, or the brain's ability to create, modify, and maintain neural pathways.

When you experience a Kundalini awakening, your thought's behavior changes, which causes you to experience drastic transformations within your brain's wiring, old patterns that were seemingly hard-wired into your mind will fade to make way for new neural pathways to take place.

Improving your brain's neuroplasticity ensures that your brain has a physical advantage when improving your mind power. A brain with healthy neuroplasticity is one that has an easier time creating and sustaining neural pathways, which means you can introduce new neural pathways that can be used to your advantage. For example, if you want to develop the habit of exercising your body regularly so you can take better care of your physical health, a brain with excellent neuroplasticity will have an easier time creating neural pathways related to exercise habits. Keeping your mind's plasticity flexible and impressionable is not as simple as choosing your thoughts, as it requires far more generous support than that. By adequately supporting your brain through mental stimulation, physical exercise, diet, overall physical health, and emotional health, you maximize your neuroplasticity to ensure that learning and creating new things is more manageable. Thus, you genuinely uncap your mind power in a physical, practical manner.

Mental Stimulation for Improved Mind Power

To grow a muscle, you need to use it. If you want to grow your biceps, for example, you would curl weights and gradually increase those weights until you have more muscular biceps. Then, you would continue curling those weights to maintain that strength. The same goes for your brain. If you want to improve your mind power, you need first to use the mind power you already have, then challenge it so that it is encouraged to grow stronger and healthier. As you continue stimulating your mind, you continue experiencing greater mind power.

There are many mentally stimulating activities you can engage in that will improve your neuroplasticity and support you with healthily creating new neural pathways. Reading, learning further information or skills, completing puzzles, using mental math, experimenting, and even using your physical body in new or unexpected ways are great opportunities to improve your neuroplasticity and increase your mind power. You must incorporate these mentally stimulating activities into your day-to-day life as often as possible, as this enables you to continuously expand your mind power. Anytime you are doing a regular daily activity, do not be afraid to do it differently, add a new skill into the mix, or unusually move your body as you do it. This unusual movement forces your brain to become more active and increases your mental flexibility around said activity, which increases your neuroplasticity and learning abilities.

Another excellent form of the mental stimulation you can engage in is Kundalini yoga or Kundalini meditation. These activities will trigger Kundalini energy to begin awakening and rising through your body and soul, which affects your entire system, including your mind. With yoga, you are priming your mind through low-impact routines that activate various forms of energy within you and create shifts within your body and mind. Meditation encourages you to use your brain in a focused, intentional manner that activates various powers while also working on your physical mind. Though both of these may seem unassuming, they have a tremendous impact on your brain's wellbeing and should be engaged with consistently.

Physical Exercise and Dietary Considerations

You are taking adequate care of your physical body aids in promoting healthy, balanced hormone levels. When your hormones are balanced, your brain has the optimal conditions for maintaining neuroplasticity and cultivating new neural pathways. Brains inundated with excess stress levels, or that lack of certain excess hormones, are less likely to function as they ought to. Inappropriate hormone levels, such as those associated with stress or other intense emotions, trigger the brain to behave differently from it normally, causing a lack of neuroplasticity or difficulty developing new neural pathways. Adequate physical exercise and a proper, healthy diet ensure that you are likely to experience optimal health, which means you experience balanced hormones that function correctly within your body.

Another benefit of physical exercise is that it not only levels out unwanted hormones and chemicals within your body but also promotes the development of hormones and chemicals that improve mental clarity and cognitive function. You should seek to get at least 30 minutes of exercise daily, while also opting to stay in motion throughout the day. Walk or bike rather than drive, take the stairs, stretch as often as you can, and spend as much time in motion as possible. If you cannot be in action, hold a robust and healthy posture, so your body thrives. Through all of this, you minimize stress and promote good health within your body, creating room for a robust and healthy brain function.

Your diet can help regulate hormones while also introducing essential nutrients to your body, which promotes good brain health. For your brain, specifically, Omega-3 fatty acids, folate, vitamin E, and flavonoids are all excellent for brain health. You can get these nutrients through nuts, fish, dark leafy greens, berries, teas, and avocados. Through these, your brain has the most effortless ability to maintain neuroplasticity and to develop new neural pathways as they are needed. With foods, just like some are beneficial, some can be harmful. Refined sugars and fats, trans fats, highly processed foods, aspartame, alcohol, and fish high in mercury can harm brain health. Avoiding all of these, while also eating more of the healthy nutrients, can improve your overall brain health so you can tap into unlimited levels of mind power. Through this, your mind truly thrives!

In ancient East Indian tradition, which Kundalini stems from, the diet was a significant factor in spiritual well being. Ayurveda, which means "The Science of Life," is a science of nutritional medicine that enabled people to balance their physical bodies to match their spiritual enlightenment. By physically treating your body with nutrition, you can adjust your earthly energy to reach your awakening soul's powers. You could also improve your soul's awakening abilities by offering it the tangible powers it needs to unite between the physical and spiritual realms.

Maintaining a Healthy Bodily Function

Focusing specifically on brain health is a natural tendency when we are discussing mind power, but it is essential to realize those other aspects of your health play into your brain's health, too. The easiest way to understand this is to recognize that your whole body is suffering anytime one part of your body is unhealthy. When you experience ill health even in one small area of your body, your brain increases your stress hormones to give your body adequate energy to correct it. Suppose you continue to experience that ailment by failing to improve your health. In that case, you continue to experience elevated stress hormones that affect your brain and the rest of your body.

Keep your blood pressure and blood sugars healthy, ensure you look after your gut health, maintain your skin health, and otherwise look after your health to maintain optimal wellbeing. Creating optimal wellbeing throughout your entire body by respecting your system as a whole ensures that your overall wellness will be strong enough to boost your mind power and keep you healthy.

Kundalini yoga is an incredible way to maintain healthy bodily function, as each pose is designed to improve the flow of energy through your body. Modern studies have shown that engaging in yoga consistently improves physical strength and the health of your hormones, muscles, joints, tendons, circulatory system, metabolism, and virtually all other processes in your body. Engaging in Kundalini yoga at least five days per week is an excellent way to reap in these benefits, while also activating your Kundalini to expand your mind power.

When engaging Kundalini yoga, it is a good idea to work alongside a trained instructor. At least, initially, Kundalini yoga is intense and triggers strong awakenings, which can be overwhelming if you are unaware of what to expect. An adequately trained instructor can help guide you through the poses and the awakening that follows, as well as any energetic experiences you might have during the process. This is highly beneficial in allowing you to enjoy your awakening healthily and powerfully to improve your experience overall.

Caring for Your Emotional Wellbeing

Beyond physical considerations, you also need to care for your emotional wellbeing. Emotions are responsible for creating various hormones and chemicals in your body, such as cortisol, dopamine, serotonin, endorphins, oxytocin, and adrenaline. If your emotions remain unchecked, your body will continue to create these hormones and chemicals, leading to you experiencing them at unhealthy levels.

Caring for your emotional wellbeing ensures that you gain relief from your triggers, which means these hormones and chemicals stop being produced in excess levels. You can return to a basic level of calm once again. You can care for your emotional well-being by being compassionate and accepting of your emotions, talking to a therapist or venting with a trusted friend, journaling, and healthily expressing yourself. You can also care for your emotional wellbeing by making choices that do not stimulate unwanted personal experiences or thinking before you act. Managing your stress and striving for balance in advance is a great way to ensure that you do not end up experiencing an excess of unexpected and unwanted emotions later on.

Those who actively work toward their enlightenment recognize that there is no such thing as "you" or "I." Instead, there is only a "we." Thus, if someone were to neglect their wellbeing, they would be expressing an apparent lack of concern for others' wellbeing. Spending time caring for your physical, mental, and emotional health ensures that you are taking proper care of your

Self so that you can express the same level of care and concern for others. This increases your capacity to experience and give love. Thus, you learn to love yourself and others more.

CHAPTER 3
A Mind-Expanding Diet

You may have caught the introduction of Ayurveda in the previous chapter, which is a topic that is essential to any discussion regarding Kundalini and mind power. According to the ancient Hindu peoples, you cannot have one without the other, so you must learn to support yourself through Ayurveda if you also wish to support yourself through Kundalini.

Ayurveda discusses topics relating to food and nutrition and recognizes them as tangible, practical ways to support our wellbeing. Hindu peoples see food as a spiritual experience, as you are assimilating your food's energy to your body, which can be either a benefit or a hindrance depending on what you are consuming. In Ayurveda, they fail to recognize a "one-size-fits-all" approach. Instead, there are three primary guidelines to follow based on your dominant dosha.

The Tridoshas

The tridoshas represent the three doshas that we each experience in our lives and bodies. The first dosha is Vata, which represents air. The second dosha is Pitta, which represents bile. The third dosha is Kapha, which represents phlegm. All three aspects of the physical self are relevant to your spiritual well being, and the metabolic processes of your body, which is why they are included in the doshas. Though the tridoshas represent aspects of the metabolic system, they are recognized as being doshas within themselves, which are life forces.

The Vata dosha is known for containing air and ether properties, and it is responsible for your energy levels. Vata also affects your movement and nerve impulses, which means breath, circulation, speech, and digestion are manifestations of the Vata dosha. If you have a Vata-dominant dosha, you are a light, enthusiastic, and creative individual. You likely have a quick-wit, and you are open to trying new experiences, especially if it means you get to stay active since you quite enjoy moving around. As a Vata-dominant, you are flexible and easy to be around, but can also be highly forgetful.

The Pitta-dominant dosha represents a well-structured person that can concentrate well and is exceptional with project management. They are always focused on practicality and leadership and love to work as teachers or guides because this allows them to spend time in their natural element. Pitta-dominant types can be more prudent with their money and other resources, as they are practical and logical in everything they do. Despite being pragmatic and focused, the Pitta type still mostly enjoys the outdoors and appreciates getting to spend energy in nature. Because of their Type-A personalities, Pitta-dominant people can be fiery and even aggressive because of the rage they often hold inside of them.

The Kapha-dominant dosha can be seen in people that are balanced, humble, and grounded. They are patient and understanding and work excellently in managerial roles to guide people without becoming overwhelmed or hot-headed by different experiences. Kapha-dominant types are also excellent with their memory and can often remember even the most minor and seemingly insignificant details of anything they experience. Routine and regularity are essential to a Kapha-dominant person, but they can lean toward habits of overeating, over-sleeping, and insufficient exercise if they are not careful.

The Types of Food

In Ayurveda, there are three types of food that you should know about: sun foods, ground foods, and earth foods. These foods provide you with different benefits, so you must regularly eat from all three categories. However, the amount you eat from each type will vary depending on which of your doshas is most dominant. Generally speaking, you want to eat fewer foods associated with your dominant dosha and more foods related to your less dominant doshas, especially favoring your least dominant dosha overall. This way, you balance your physical energy to your spiritual life, which is believed to help your enlightenment.

Sun foods are any foods that grow well above the ground, such as fruits. Eating plenty of fruits will give you the bright, fiery energy of the sun, which helps liven up your personal power and bring you closer to enlightenment.

Ground foods grow close to the ground, such as grains, vegetables, and low-growing fruits like strawberries. Ground foods are excellent for cleansing your body and energy and keeping you grounded in your Self and Spirit.

Earth foods are those that grow beneath the ground, such as root vegetables. Consuming earth foods is excellent for helping heal your body and energy, so consume them regularly. It is always a good idea to consume a wide range of colors when you eat the sun, ground, and earth foods to ensure that you are getting the best energy intake possible, so eat the rainbow!

Eating for Your Doshas

Eating for your dosha depends on which dosha is your dominant one. You can identify your dominant dosha by taking a simple Ayurveda test online, which will allow you to discover which of your doshas is most prevalent and which is least. From there, you can eat your diet accordingly to help balance your dominant dosha and elevate your least dominant one.

If you have a Vata-dominant dosha, you must eat cooked vegetables, well-ripened fruits, dairy, small amounts of poultry or seafood, sweeteners, and grains. It is important to avoid using spices in large quantities and avoid bitter and astringent herbs, as they will not work well with your dosha type.

Vata-dominant doshas should eat:

- Almonds
- Apricots
- Asparagus
- Avocados
- Bananas
- Beets
- Berries
- Carrots
- Chicken
- Chickpeas
- Cherries
- Coconut
- Cucumber

- Dairy (all)
- Figs
- Garlic
- Ghee
- Grapefruit
- Grapes
- Green beans
- Lemons
- Mangoes
- Mung beans
- Olive oil
- Onions
- Papaya
- Peaches
- Pineapple
- Pink lentils
- Plums
- Seafood
- Sesame oil
- Sour oranges
- Stewed fruits
- Sweet melons
- Sweet potatoes
- Radishes
- Tofu
- Turkey
- Turnips

In moderation, Vata-dominant types can eat:

- Barely
- Black beans

- Broccoli
- Brussels sprouts
- Buckwheat
- Cabbage
- Cauliflower
- Celery
- Corn
- Cranberries
- Eggplant
- Kidney beans
- Leafy green vegetables
- Millet
- Mushrooms
- Peas
- Pears
- Peppers
- Pomegranates
- Potatoes
- Red meat
- Sprouts
- Tomatoes
- Wheat
- Zucchini

Vata-dominant types should avoid eating:

- Astringent herbs and spices
- Bitter herbs and spices
- Dried fruits
- Unripe fruits

If you have a Pitta-dominant dosha, anything that has a bitter, sweet, or astringent taste is best, as well as cold or warm foods. Because your dosha indicates that you are fiery and passionate, it makes sense that you need cooler foods to help you balance your fire energy.

Pitta-dominant doshas should eat:

- Asparagus
- Avocado
- Bananas
- Barley
- Broccoli
- Brussels sprouts
- Butter
- Cabbage
- Carrots
- Cauliflower
- Celery
- Cherries
- Chicken
- Chickpeas
- Coconut
- Cucumber
- Egg whites
- Figs
- Flaxseeds
- Ghee
- Grapeseed oil
- Green beans
- Green peppers
- Leafy green vegetables
- Lettuce
- Mangoes
- Melons

- Milk
- Mung beans
- Mushrooms
- Oats
- Okra
- Olive oil
- Oranges
- Parsley
- Pears
- Peas
- Pineapples
- Plums
- Potatoes
- Prunes
- Pumpkin seeds
- Radishes
- Raisins
- Red lentils
- River fish
- Shrimp
- Spinach
- Sprouts
- Squash
- Sunflower oil
- Sunflower seeds
- Sweet potatoes
- Tofu
- Turkey
- Wheat
- White rice
- Zucchini

In moderation, Pitta-dominant types can eat:

- Almond oil
- Apricot
- Apples
- Ar har Dal
- Beets
- Berries
- Black gram
- Black lentils
- Brown rice
- Cheese
- Chiles
- Coconut oil
- Corn
- Corn oil
- Dark grapes
- Eggplants
- Egg yolk
- Grapefruit
- Hot peppers
- Ice cream
- Millet
- Onions
- Peaches
- Persimmons
- Pineapples
- Raw papaya
- Red meat
- Rye
- Safflower oil
- Seafood
- Sesame oil
- Sour buttermilk

- Sour cherries
- Sour cream
- Sour yogurt
- Tomatoes

Pitta-dominant types should avoid eating:

- Fermented foods
- Honey
- Molasses
- Spices

If you have a Kapha-dominant dosha, you must favor warm, light, and dry foods. Lightly cooked meals are excellent, too, though you should select eating as much raw food as possible to balance your energy. Spicy food is ideal for Kapha-dominant doshas, also, so enjoy as much spicy food as you want!

Kapha-dominant doshas should eat:

- Almond oil
- Apples
- Apricots
- Asparagus
- Barley
- Basmati rice
- Beans (all types)
- Beets
- Berries
- Broccoli
- Brussels sprouts
- Buckwheat
- Cabbage

- Camel milk
- Carrots
- Cauliflower
- Celery
- Cherries
- Chicken
- Corn
- Cranberries
- Dried fruits
- Eggs
- Eggplant
- Flaxseeds
- Garlic
- Goats milk
- Grapefruits
- Grapeseed oil
- Leafy green vegetables
- Lean fish
- Lettuce
- Millet
- Mushrooms
- Oats
- Okra
- Olive oil
- Onions
- Papaya
- Pears
- Peas
- Peppers
- Pomegranate
- Potatoes
- Prunes
- Pumpkin seeds

- Radishes
- Rye
- Skim milk
- Soy milk
- Spices (all)
- Spinach
- Sprouts
- Sunflower oil
- Sunflower seeds
- Turkey

In moderation, Kapha-dominant types can eat:

- Bananas
- Coconuts
- Cucumbers
- Dates
- Egg yolks
- Fresh figs
- Kidney beans
- Mangoes
- Red meat
- Rice
- Shrimp
- Sweet potatoes
- Tofu
- Tomatoes
- Wheat
- Zucchini

Kapha-dominant types should avoid eating:

- Hot cereals

- Steamed grains

CHAPTER 4
Yoga And Mind Power

Kundalini yoga is one of the primary ways to connect to spirit, activate your life force energy, and trigger your enlightenment. From the outside, Kundalini yoga looks like a series of exercises and postures to move the physical body. However, the reality of what is going on lies far more profound than mere physical movements. When engaged in Kundalini yoga, you are also involved in deep meditation, which allows you to activate your energy and awaken your Kundalini. Yoga will both facilitate the awakening and guide you through balancing and relaxing your awakened powers. This is the optimal way to integrate your life for a deeper connection to higher self and consciousness.

The Snake in Your Spine

In Kundalini, it is said that your life force energy coils around your spine and, upon activating, "slithers" up your spine and out your crown chakra like a snake uncoiling and slithering away from a branch. When you activate your energy, you are likely to see and feel this energy moving up through your body and awakening each of your chakras along the way.

Even after your initial awakening, you will continue to experience imagery and energy as your life force energy routinely uncoils and awakens even further, and moves through your chakras with greater consistency. Throughout your day to day life, your Kundalini energy will gradually relax back into the base of your spine, so regular yoga practices are essential to release this energy and promote healing and awakening.

White and Kundalini Yoga

Kundalini yoga classes are chock full of people wearing white. Wearing white is essential, as colors are said to create an uncontrollable action within your subconscious mind, which affects your productivity, inspiration, and expansion. Since you want to be deeply engaged in your session, you do not wish to have the distracting effects of colors taking away from your experience, which is why practitioners commonly wear white.

Tuning in for Your Session

Before every session, you must start by tuning in. Tuning in allows you to become aware of your energy, connect to your higher self, and connect to higher powers. To clear and neutralize your mind means to release the five causes of unhappiness: lust, anger, greed, pride, and attachment. When you remove these from your consciousness and deeply tune into your energy field, you gain the ability to experience more peace and harmony in all areas of your life.

Tuning in is achieved by chanting *Ong Namo Guru Dev Namo* as you remain seated with your hands over your heart center in prayer pose. This mantra translates to "bowing to the truth within you; your relationship to your own destiny."

Kundalini Kriyas and Mantra

Once you are tuned in, you can commence your Kundalini yoga session with Kriyas and mantras. Kriyas are the practices you will follow, while mantras incite Kundalini yoga's meditation aspect so you can achieve higher consciousness through your session. In this way, you unite your physical and spiritual elements to create a whole-body experience.

The kriyas you fulfill will be done from a seated position. Start by extending your arms above your head and shaking them, as well as your entire upper body and your head. This shaking releases fear, anxiety, and other pent-up emotions from your body so you can experience freedom from the tension and overwhelm.

Next, you can move into a shoulder stand. If you are capable, a shoulder stand can be accomplished by rolling up through your spine and straightening your legs straight above you as you lean upon your shoulders. If you can do this properly and maintain it, it is said that a 15-minute shoulder stand is the equivalent of sleeping for 2 hours.

Seated rock pose is an excellent Kundalini kriya to use. You can enter this pose by sitting with your shins tucked under you. Then, bring your hands to your shoulders with your elbows out wide and keep your spine straight and tall. Inhale, then turn to the left, exhale and turn to the right. Your spine should remain in the same place vertically, though it should be rotating left and right with each inhale and exhale.

Deep squats can be done by keeping your hands at your heart in prayer pose. You should keep your spine straight and tall, too. Bend at your knees, dropping your bottom toward the ground, but keep your head upright. As you lower, inhale, and as you come back up, exhale.

Finally, spinal flexion is a great move that can be achieved by sitting in a cross-legged position. You want to move your chest forward but keep your head still, then move your chest backward while still keeping your head in the same place. Your arms should be moving with you as you move back and forth. This helps open your diaphragm and chest, as well as your shoulders.

The mantra you can say as you engage in Kundalini yoga practice is "Sa Ta Na Ma." These sounds represent the universe's five primal sounds: infinity, life, death and transformation, and rebirth. Chant them to yourself following your kriyas to activate these energies within your being and expand your mind power.

CHAPTER 5
Relationships And Mind Power

If you truly want to unlock any power within yourself, it pays to spend time researching historical humans and the way we once were. Understanding our species' history allows you to understand the nature of who you are, which enables you to tap into the power of instinct and primal urges. Historically speaking, humans have always been a tribal species, meaning we thrive with connection and being close to others of our own kind. We also thrive when we have interspecies relationships, such as the ones we share with our dogs, cats, and other beloved family pets. However, relationships with our own kind are optimal as they enable us to feel received, connected, safe, and accepted by our own kind. They are indeed essential to our wellbeing.

Beyond the physical benefits you gain from thriving relationships, it has also been shown that you gain extensive value spiritually. Your relationships add energy to your life and can impact your power, too. When you engage in high-quality, thriving relationships with people who support you with elevating your energy and wellbeing, you further awaken your own energy field and increase your enlightenment. The people we surround ourselves by can heavily encourage us, causing us to take our own enlightenment more seriously, too, which can inspire you to work more persistently toward activating the entirety of your mind power.

Extensive evidence from modern research has shown that humans thrive on high-quality relationships with other humans, as they allow us to live longer, happier lives. Those who have healthy relationships with other humans are known for having fewer mental health problems because their brains are functioning in the best possible manner. When you have close, positive relationships with others, you gain a sense of purpose and find yourself feeling as though you belong, all of which have a positive impact on your brain's health, and therefore your mind power.

Loneliness and isolation are two conditions that have grown in the technology era, mainly because people are primarily nurturing relationships behind screens rather than face to face. Though it does create a sense of connection, it is not the same as the one you experience when you are in physical contact with someone, or at the very least, when you can see them face to face. As humans, we have something called a mirror neuron, which is responsible for us feeling close and connected with other humans. Essentially, when we behave in some way or observe someone else acting somehow, the mirror neuron is enabled, and we begin to recognize similarities between ourselves and others. Those similarities lead to empathy, compassion, deeper bonds, and a meaningful sense of belonging. When we do not spend enough time around other people, our neurons do not fire, and we fail that tangible sense of connection with others.

The other side of this is that, when we fail to have healthy relationships with others, we fail to feel a sense of belonging, which leads to less real psychological issues that are still just as serious. Reduced self-esteem, a lack of self-confidence, and disorders such as anxiety, depression, and even individual personality disorders can all be triggered when we feel as though we do not belong with our "tribe." If you truly want to tap into your unlimited mind power, you must focus on nurturing healthy, positive relationships in your life.

Creating Strong Relationships in Your Life

Creating healthy relationships in your life is something we are all intended to learn as children, but it doesn't always go as planned. Learning how to build healthy, stable relationships in adulthood takes practice. Still, it can become a skill that you are strong with, which means it becomes easier for you to create and enjoy healthy relationships with fellow adults.

There are five significant steps you can take toward developing strong relationships in your life: give time, be present, listen, be listened to, and recognize unhealthy relationships.

Giving time to your relationships is one of the most powerful things you can do, though it might feel impossible if your schedule is continually packed with things to do. You might find that you are so invested in your career and your family that making time for your friends seems challenging, so it becomes a low priority. You must realize the importance of these relationships and commit time to them, even when it seems challenging, so that you can invest in your relationships in a healthy manner.

Being present is an essential step to building relationships, as it allows you to ensure that you are entirely in the moment with those you are spending time with. When you do carve out time for your friends or family, be sure that you are entirely available and that you are enjoying that time with them. Put your phone away, stop giving mental energy to issues you are dealing with elsewhere, and allow yourself to become fully present in that moment. Enjoy the time you are spending with your loved ones, as this presence massively deepens the connection you share by having each of you invested in developing your relationship with each other, rather than with distractions.

Listening is one of the best things you can do when nurturing relationships, especially as an adult. As children, we do not worry about listening to our peers because we are all so preoccupied with our own experiences. As adults, we thrive when those around us hear us. Listen to what your friends are saying in a non-judgmental way, and concentrate on their needs when they are talking. Allow yourself to truly hear about your friends, who they are, and what they are experiencing, and witness how this deepens your bond as you come to understand your friend even more.

Being listened to is another valuable asset to any budding relationship. You might feel as though you should hold things in, hide certain aspects of your personality, or otherwise contour who you are to meet the needs of someone else. Especially in adulthood, relationships, where such nonsense is expected, should not be maintained. Be honest, authentic, and clear; allow others to receive you and support you as you are. This shows those you are sharing a relationship with that you are also willing to be open, which allows them to feel comfortable opening up around you.

Lastly, you need to be able to recognize and eliminate unhealthy relationships from your life. Relationships where you are always listening, always talking, people are manipulating you, negativity or drama seeps in, or other toxic behaviors are ruling should always be eliminated. You can be seriously affected mentally, emotionally, and even physically when you are in unhealthy relationships, as they are incredibly harmful. Recognizing the harm of these situations can help you move forward healthily by either resolving the toxicity in the relationship or dissolving the relationship altogether.

Using Relationships as a Point of Growth

Beyond offering you a chance to bond with others and experience a deepened sense of belonging and connection, relationships can offer many impressive points of growth. The increase you feel in your personal value and self-confidence and self-esteem will have a significant impact on your wellbeing; however, you can become even more intentional inside your relationships to use them as a significant growing point in your life.

One excellent way relationships help you grow is by increasing your sense of trust in yourself. When you realize that you are an emotionally dependable person and capable of adding value to other people's lives, it allows you to see yourself as a positive, wholesome individual. When you realize that you can support others, you stop feeling timid in relationships and your life because you know you can benefit yourself, and others, in a positive manner.

Another great way to intentionally grow through your relationships is to use them to learn about yourself and use them as an opportunity to learn in general. To learn about yourself, relationships offer you the ability to understand how you relate to others and what you need in a relationship to feel valued and supported. You also learn about how you can behave in a healthier manner inside of relationships by recognizing how you can support others with having their needs met and how you can have your needs met inside each relationship. It can be incredibly powerful to understand the role friendship plays versus the role an acquaintanceship or romantic relationship plays in your life and to discover how to fulfill your needs and the needs of others within each relationship. Through this, you effectively increase your independence while also improving the level of connection you share with others, which creates an excellent learning opportunity.

When it comes to learning from others directly, relationships of all varieties can provide you with the opportunity to see things from different perspectives. As you get to know your friends, acquaintances, or romantic partners, you get to know what their points of view are on the world, and how these may influence you to grow your point of view. This expanding point of view may help you with personal issues, or it may allow you to understand others better so you can deepen your compassion and expand the value of your relationships. Either way, you will be developing your mind power as your cup overflows with support, understanding, knowledge, and experience.

How Relationships Affect Your Spiritual Energy

Relationships can either add to or take away from your wellbeing. Even seemingly neutral relationships will either add or take away, depending on where they fall on the benefits spectrum. When you are in negative relationships, it shows how your energy feels and how you show up in life. Negative associations will drain your energy, negatively influence you, and leave you feeling as though you are continually adjusting yourself or cleansing your energy field from chaos. The more you experience these types of drama and chaos in your relationships, the more you find yourself struggling to support your enlightenment because you are getting caught up with too much "yuck" on earth.

Positive relationships, on the other hand, can drastically improve the quality of your life. When you are surrounded by people that take their energy seriously, work toward their enlightenment, and routinely improve upon themselves, you can feel it. You feel empowered and uplifted when you are around them, can enjoy greater feelings of growth, and you are motivated to stay on track with your personal development. These positive relationships are beneficial, making you far more likely to enjoy your awakening and feel balanced and empowered in your life.

CHAPTER 6
The Number One Mind Power Killer

If you truly want to transform your life's quality and expand your mind power beyond your wildest beliefs, you *must* eliminate the number one mind power killer from your life. This killer often lurks in the shadows, silently sneaking in and finding ways to decimate your sense of confidence and wellbeing. It will destroy your mind power and your physical wellbeing, and the quality of your life as a whole.

The trouble with this killer is that every one of us faces it, as it is a natural part of life. In fact, in small doses and under control, the killer is actually an assistant and can support you in many different ways. However, most people experience out-of-control relationships with this killer, which is why it has the capacity to become so toxic and destroy the wellbeing of so many.

The Secret Killer of Mind Power…

The secret killer of mind power is lurking in your everyday life. You experience it frequently, likely even daily. If you are ahead of the game, you have already found a way to identify and stop the killer in its tracks, but if you are not, you are likely still struggling with it regularly. You experience the killer anytime you receive unexpected news, your boss tightens a deadline on a project you were already late for, your to-do list gets too long, or you have to do something you do not want to do. The secret killer of mind power is also known as *stress*.

When it is in balance, stress gives you that little boost of energy you need to get things done. Stress can be helpful in the immediate moment, or as a short-term motivator that supplies the energy and mental focus you need to achieve anything you desire. When it isn't in balance, or you experience it for a prolonged period of time, stress creates more problems than it solves. Over time, your heightened focus becomes anxiety, excess energy becomes problematic, and emotional pressure begins to feel burdensome to the point of overwhelm and burnout. If you do not keep your stress in check, it *will* cause many problems, including a significant decrease in your mind power.

How This Killer Affects Your Energy

Stress is a form of energy that encourages contractions. Think about it: anytime you are stressed, your muscles tense, and you shrink into yourself. You might even feel smaller because of how much the stress is weighing on you; when you contract, even physically, due to an emotional trigger, your energy contracts, too. As your energy contracts, your Kundalini contracts, and you reduce your awakened energies. You might even find yourself feeling completely disconnected, closed, or off-center due to the contraction.

Relieving yourself of stress is essential if you want to expand your energies to enjoy your awakening once more. Understand that you will often come across stress in your life, and every time it will cause contractions and minimize your energy. It is helpful to become aware of this to remain consistent in observing and recovering from these contractions. Consistency in this part of your life will help keep you open, receptive, and fluid and strengthen your resiliency and ability to bounce back from stressful experiences.

How to Spot the Killer

Finding the root causes of stress in your life is imperative if you will overthrow this energy and free up your mind power for more important things, like creating your dream life. Identifying stress in your life is most effective if you can discover the triggers that cause you to feel stressed in the first place to find ways to eliminate these triggers. The easiest way to locate your stress triggers is to locate the areas in your life where you feel a lack of mind power. In other words, where do you feel as though you cannot grow, or as though you have zero inspiration or energy to make a change to that area of your life?

Any area in your life where you feel as though you are struggling, or like there is no chance for you to grow or change that area of your life, is an area where you feel stressed. The reality is, you can grow and transform any location of your life, regardless of what struggles you are facing, though excess stress can make the idea of change seem impossible.

Some everyday stress triggers include:

- Fear of failure
- Fear of speaking in front of a crowd
- Fear of judgment

- Uncertainty or a lack of control
- Beliefs
- Your attitudes, opinions, or expectations

It is a good idea to brainstorm all of your likely stressors and rate them from 0-10, with 10 being the most stressful thing you could imagine. Once you know what your stressors are, it becomes a lot easier to witness them and take action so that stress is no longer a significant threat to your wellbeing or your mind power.

What to Do About It

After identifying your triggers, you must use this information to your advantage. Stress left unchecked presents a serious issue, so you must discover how you can use this information to manage existing stress and prevent future triggers from causing such significant stress in your life. Once you can manage stress in these areas, you open room for you to expand your mind power in them, enabling you to experience unparalleled growth that assists you with reaching your next level.

Before you can prepare yourself against your triggers being pulled in the future, you must learn to release and manage the stress you have accumulated from the triggers. Thoroughly releasing existing tension ensures that you approach your triggers from the point of peace, which means keeping your stress low is much more comfortable.

An excellent way to reduce immediate stress you are facing is through biofeedback. Biofeedback is a process that occurs when your body experiences a trigger that tells your brain something is wrong, effectively triggering a bout of stress. If you have been experiencing ongoing stress, the biofeedback you are likely encountering at the moment includes rapid breath, a quickened heart rate, tense muscles, and difficulty with eating or sleeping. You are essentially experiencing symptoms relating to the fight or flight mode, which is triggering your body to remain fixated on stress. Using biofeedback to reverse engineer your emotional state requires you to intentionally relax all of your stressful symptoms, so your brain receives the message that "it is okay." Relax your muscles, remove your tongue from the roof of your mouth, slow your breathing rate, eat something slowly, and give yourself time to bring calm into your body intentionally. Meditating is a great way to get relaxation into your body during a time of stress, as it provides you with the opportunity to bring peace to every aspect of your being without rejecting or forcing the pressure out of your body.

Once your body begins to experience relief from stress, you can start using your mindset to release more. The easiest way to rapidly shift your perspective on stress is to recognize stress as a natural symptom of difficult experiences. It is a temporary experience that you can seek relief from. After you have shifted your perspective around stress itself, you can move your viewpoint around the trigger that is causing you to feel stressed in the first place. Going your view around a trigger is best accomplished if you focus on creating acceptance around your motivation, rather than eliminating the trigger. This will earn you rapid results, whereas removing triggers often takes a significant amount of exposure before you start to feel any relief from those triggers.

When you know you will be facing one of your stress triggers, it can help you start engaging in the biofeedback process well in advance, so you are ready to face those triggers more peacefully. You may feel the first several times as though the biofeedback is not working because your body is used to reacting to those triggers with stress. As you continue using this approach, however, your body will begin to respond to these triggers in a more relaxed manner, which means you will be able to navigate them without such significant reactions.

Protecting Yourself From It

Protecting yourself against further stress may seem like an impossible feat, and in a sense, it is. You cannot prevent yourself from ever feeling pressure again, nor can you stop troubling things from happening to you; however, you can protect yourself by having a plan for how you will deal with stress in the future.

Part of protecting yourself against stress ensures you have optimal physical health, so your body is prepared to endure stressors as they arise. When your body is in optimal health, experiencing increased adrenaline or cortisol is not as bothersome because you are not already experiencing underlying stress due to poor health. As a result, you have more resilience toward additional stress in your life.

Another way to protect yourself against stress is to have a consistent stress management routine you use no matter what has triggered your tension. A great response to stress would be to take a breathing break, relax your muscles, and give yourself a few moments to experience calmness before facing the trigger, causing your stress. The more you repeat this healthy habit for stress management, the sooner you will experience relief from any form of stress you experience in your life.

CHAPTER 7
The Mindset Aspects Of Mind Power

When your mindset's physical foundation has been laid, the next step to building out your mind power lies in your mindset. The particularly impressive thing about mindset is that, regardless of how healthy your brain is, you will not have full access to your mind power if you do not have the right mindset. You can increase your mind power by accessing the right attitude, which enables you to create anything you desire, whether it be a specific result, a great day, or the fulfillment of a long-term goal.

You can take multiple steps to create a mindset that allows you to tap into the full extent of your mind power. From rapidly sorting through information to decide what is worth your attention and what is not, to look at what your mental patterns are and how you can use them to your advantage, there are many ways you can use your mindset to your advantage.

Awakening your Kundalini energy means you will inevitably experience a complete shift in your mindset. As soon as these energies awaken, you will start seeing yourself, others, the world around you, and the universe in a different light. Suddenly, things that once bothered you or negatively affected you will seem entirely irrelevant, and something that was once beyond your awareness will become imperative for you to focus on. You will find yourself naturally shifting into these more significant mindsets that improve your wellbeing and keep you growing toward your enlightenment.

Taking complete control over your mindset requires patience, consistency, and commitment. You have to be willing to continually work toward improving your mood for as long as it takes, regardless of how slow your results may be. The more you work toward improving your attitude with relentless consistency, the stronger your foundation will be, and the better your perspective will be overall.

How Mindset Controls Your Mind Power

Your mindset controls your mind power by telling you how to use your mind power. Regardless of how you use your perspective or not, your mind power exists. However, a person with a negative mindset is not acknowledging or tapping into their mind power. Instead, they ignore it or make excuses for why they are incapable of tapping into it, which results in them not taking action on the power they already have.

If you take the time to cultivate a healthy mindset, you give yourself the ability to acknowledge your power and use it to your advantage. You realize that there is no difference between you, Tony Robbins, Oprah Winfrey, massive government head figures, wildly successful CEOs, or anyone else who has achieved anything you desire. The same power they had to create the results they made exists within you, and you can use that power to achieve anything you want in life.

Just like they could transform their mindset, you also can change your mindset. With the right consistency, intention, and desire, you can manifest anything you wish in your life, and you can start it by imagining it, using the creative powers of your mind, and working toward it with consistency.

The Mindset That Unlocks Your Potential

The mindset that unlocks your potential is simple yet life-changing. It is rooted in a straightforward question, and with this question, you can achieve anything you desire in life. The problem is: "How can I do this?"

From a base state of being, when the average majority decides they want something in life, their initial reaction is to say "too bad," or "that's not possible." They always think something along the lines of why it would never happen, or how everything could go wrong to prevent them from getting their desired results. What they never think is, "How can I do this?" or "How can I make this happen?"

Immediately upon asking this question, you must start legitimately searching for the answers. Activate your creative power and look for ways that you could start turning the results you desire. Some of your responses may seem elaborate, impossible, or completely unreasonable, while others will seem like they could be possible. The ones that seem like they could be possible, and like they would likely get you the results you desire, are the ones you want to focus on. These are the ones that can get you the results you need and want and transform your life.

Awakening Your Kundalini Mindsets

As you awaken Kundalini, you will awaken your "Kundalini mindsets," or mindsets that are commonly seen in those that activate their energy field. The most significant change you will observe is a transformation in what you think about, and how. Suddenly, matters of the physical world will seem irrelevant to you. You no longer worry about things like poverty, lack, failure, or other commonly feared things, because you know that these are all trivial matters that cannot be healed through worry or fear. Things that used to bother you, like how someone else treated you, what they thought of you, or the circumstances you presently face, no longer matter because you realize they are not relevant to your wellbeing. The only thing relevant to your wellbeing is you and your beliefs, as well as the way you treat yourself.

You will likely find yourself starting to believe that you must treat others better and have compassion for others' journeys, as a way to show love to yourself. The kinder you are to others, and the less you concern yourself with them, the more at peace you will be in your life. Integrating these new, higher consciousness mindsets is essential to your awakening and enlightenment, so it is crucial to become aware of them and incorporate them into your life as they arise.

Incorporating a New Mindset Into Your Life

Incorporating a new mindset into your life is a work of art in and of itself. It would be best if you transformed the way you think about *everything*. A person that embraces a negative state of mind will think negatively about everything, and you must change that within yourself if you wish to unleash your mind power. You must stop thinking negatively about the commute to work, the food you eat, the people in your life, the music on the radio, the way someone looked at you, the weather, and everything else in your life. There is no room for you to think negatively about anything, as even a small amount of negative thinking can block your positive results.

Incorporate your positive thinking into everything, even that which seems completely irrelevant. Think positively about the people in the other cars, your coworkers, the weather, and the world around you. Even when everything seems to be going wrong, or it seems as though you have plenty to be cynical about, choose to be positive instead. Embracing positivity in all areas of your life, no matter how small, insignificant, or challenging it may seem, enables you to improve your mindset overall by incorporating a positive-oriented perspective into your everyday life. This way, when more significant circumstances arise, or you find yourself in need of your positive thinking skills, you have them to rely on because you have been building them in your everyday life.

CHAPTER 8
Having A Growth Mindset

A growth mindset is a term that defines one's ability to see opportunity over a lack of opportunity. When you have a growth mindset, you are naturally more willing to search for ways to overcome obstacles or opportunities to create something magnificent in your life. Even if you struggle with specific weaknesses or have experienced a setback in any area of your life, you believe that you can share something positive. So you routinely work toward bringing more positive into your life. Having a growth mindset is essential if you will embrace your mind power's full capacity, so it is essential that you work toward improving your growth mindset every day.

Growth Mindset Vs. Fixed Mindset

A growth mindset is the opposite of a fixed mindset. A growth mindset means you are looking for growth and change opportunities, while a fixed mindset means that you reject the idea change could happen. People with a fixed mindset believe everything is based on luck, there is no hope for them to experience anything different than their "fate," and they will never have the power to create anything better for themselves in their lives. If you have a fixed mindset, you block your capacity to receive your natural mind power because you refuse to acknowledge it and use it to your advantage.

Some suggest that if you have a fixed mindset, there is no way that you can move out of that. In other words, you either have a fixed mindset or a growth mindset, and you can't change which you have. Fortunately, you can feel confident that you have a growth mindset, as you are here reading this book and accepting the fact that there is a chance you could change the things you do not like about your life. In other words, you have hope. That, right there, is a critical indicator that you have a growth mindset.

In order to nurture your growth mindset and gain even more from it, there are many things you can do to expand that growth mentality and access an abundance of your mind power. You should do at least one of the following ten things every single day to expand your mind power and experience change in your life.

Kundalini and Growth Mindset

As you have discovered, many things that affect your physical and practical wellbeing affect your spiritual well being, too. The same remains true for the growth mindset and Kundalini. Simply put, one cannot fully tap into their Kundalini awakening if they are determined to believe that their present circumstances are the only thing they are capable of. It would help if you believed that you have some level of power over your wellbeing to enable yourself to lean in when you feel your awakening. Failing to lean in, or continually work toward awakening your energies, can lead to you sabotaging your awakening or contracting your powers.

Many times, people who believe awakening is a lie or that carry skepticism in spirituality and spiritual energies have a fixed mindset. Their fixed mindset leads them to think that no such thing is possible, so despite their efforts to awaken, they never actually awaken or activate their energy because they cannot let go. You must be willing to lean into your growth mindset and your awakening if you experience the full power of Kundalini in your life. Below are some excellent steps you can take to cultivate your growth mindset to further activate your Kundalini energy.

Be Conscious About What You Feed Your Mind

You must do every day of your life and be conscious of what you are feeding your mind. The thoughts you think to yourself, and the content you consume from the world around you are all feeding your mindset. If you are continually thinking negative things to yourself or feeding into your fears, you block your growth mindset and prevent yourself from tapping into your fullest capacity. Likewise, if you are consuming negative news, following people you dislike, or regularly talking to negative people, you are wasting your mind power on self-limiting negativity. Unfollow accounts that do not support your growth; speak to yourself in an empowering manner and avoid news or people routinely feeding you with negative information. When you are conscious about the content you consume and how you speak to yourself, you provide yourself with the range you need to grow, rather than shrink.

Work on Your Desire

Your mind is full of desires, and there are plenty of passions you could be pursuing right now. Unlike other goals, you truly desire built-in motivation because you are already eager to turn results out of those goals. Your desire, in and of itself, is motivating. The more you work toward fulfilling your desires and creating more passion in your life, the more you support yourself with achieving a positive outcome in life. Even if you do not presently have any goals associated with your desires, explore your passions, and create skills surrounding your desires. The more you sink into a passion and fill your life with it, the more you will develop goals that genuinely fuel you, and have the motivation to fulfill those goals, too.

Have the Right Sources

A lack of knowledge can prevent you from moving forward in your life because you genuinely do not know how to. No matter how much you might consider possible routes to success, if you do not know actually to put a foot on the pavement and turn results, it can block you from doing anything with that desire. Ensure that you access adequate resources to learn about the necessary tools to fulfill your desires and then use that knowledge to help move you forward. Any resource you access for learning should be one that promotes your ideas and encourages you to create your desired results; otherwise, you are not following your desires.

Embrace a Drive to Learn

If you have reached a point in your life where you have become relatively comfortable with mediocrity, it is time to change that. You need to embrace a drive to learn, and that hunger for knowledge should be as massive as you can keep it. To incorporate a lesson that Grant Cardone routinely teaches his followers, consider your current thirst for knowledge, and 10x it. In other words, blow it up to ten times the size of your present need, and aim to fulfill *that* drive, rather than the one you are presently working with. The more you can drive yourself to get excited and learn more, the greater your knowledge will be, and the stronger your results, too.

Stay Open and Flexible

Life will never go as you planned it. Fear and negative self-talk will hold you back, but they are not the only things that will hold you back. If you are unwilling to take steps forward because you are rigid in how you believe it should happen, or you are not open to the idea of change, you are blocking your mind power. Mind power occurs when you are flexible, honest, and willing to embrace change as it is needed. As you discover new knowledge or information, you will find that your understanding of how things should be done will change, too. Staying flexible ensures that you can seamlessly move into a new path and continue growing toward your desires, rather than remaining trapped in a current path that is not optimal or functional.

Be Creative and Successful

If you can imagine yourself with happiness at any point in the future, be creative enough to imagine yourself being happy now, and allow yourself to experience that success in the present. Far too many people believe that their happiness exists in the next milestone and believe that thanks to their mind power, they will be able to achieve that milestone successfully, and then they will feel good. Unfortunately, this keeps you from feeling good in the present, which keeps you from achieving your desired results. That's right: feeling good is a significant part of activating your mind power and creating your desired results. Allow yourself to feel good about who you are and where you are at right now and use that positive energy to fuel you to do even better. In the long run, this is a far more sustainable approach than always placing your happiness in the hands of the future.

Release Others' Influence Over You

Our modern world mostly relies on the influence of others. People affect us about what to like, what to buy, where to vacation, what jobs to aspire to, what interests to have, and everything else you can imagine. Being influenced is not necessarily bad, but being blindly influenced is not useful to your wellbeing. You must release others' influence over you if you have ultimate control over your own life and wellbeing. This means that you should not only tune out significant influencers such as those we see on social media and in Hollywood, but also the private influencers you have in your own life, too. Tune out the sound of family, friends, and anyone else who is attempting to influence you, especially if their influence does not lead you to create the results you desire. Focus only on yourself and what you want, and let everything else fade into the background. In other words, become your influencer.

An excellent way to gain control over yourself and eliminate others' influence over you is to engage in mindfulness. A daily mindfulness practice will allow you to check-in with yourself, identify where you have been authentic and where you have been influenced, and come back to your personal center. There, you can make choices intentionally and have a greater level of control over yourself.

The best way to implement a mindfulness practice into your daily routine is to have periodic check-ins, as well as the end of day reviews. During your periodic check-ins, you will simply be doing a quick mental check-in with yourself. Each hour, spend 1-2 minutes observing how you feel, what you are thinking about, and how you are behaving. If you recognize any area with unwanted influence, adjust how you approach that area, so you are in alignment with yourself and your genuine desire. During your end of day reviews, you want to go deeper. Bring out your journal, relax, and write down all of the significant choices you made in your day, and why. This is an excellent opportunity to reflect on what influenced you throughout the day, and whether or not you were consciously or subconsciously influenced. If you realize you were subconsciously influenced, that is a great opportunity to review how the influence occurred and bring awareness to this area of your life so you can refrain from experiencing such influence in the future. This way, you regain conscious control over yourself and your wellbeing.

Surround Yourself With Positivity

As with releasing people's influence over you, it can be useful to surround yourself with people and materials that will influence you in a positive manner. Surround yourself with people who are also interested in unlocking their mind power, increasing their growth mindset, and stepping into their fullest potential. As well, focus on consuming more materials that are positive and that encourage you to think, feel, and experience life in a way that aligns with your desires. For example, rather than scrolling social media, scroll through a book that serves your growth mindset and encourages you to create the results you desire in life. The more you surround yourself with what you want to become, the more you will influence yourself to become that person.

Speak of Present Success

One of the key tools of manifesting that warrants people's rapid results is their ability to speak in the present tense. The purpose of speaking in the present tense is not to serve some woo-woo idea that doing so magically affords you the results you desire. Rather, doing so ensures that you are focused on bringing your desires into your reality *right now*. Saying "I am getting fit" is far more ambitious and focused than saying, "I will get fit." When you say "I am getting fit," your brain becomes fixated on how you can actively get fit right now. The same goes for everything you desire. Rather than saying "I will" or "one day," say "I am" and "right now." This transition in your language is incredibly transformational and will encourage your growth mindset to kick in and start looking for ways to manifest your desires as soon as possible.

Work Through Your Resistance

Regardless of how consistently you work toward building your growth mindset, you will experience resistance. You will experience fear, doubts, negativity, and even levels of resistance that you cannot explain. At times, you might even find yourself procrastinating with no clear reason as to why you are procrastinating because that which you are avoiding doing is something you are genuinely interested in. Still, you cannot seem to get yourself in motion. Whenever you experience resistance, refrain from automatically saying, "oh well, too bad, I guess I don't want it bad enough." Instead, ask yourself, "How can I do this?" "How can I work through this resistance and create my desired results?" "How can I make this happen?"

CHAPTER 9
Deepening Your Sense Of Self

There are many theories as to what a "self" is. During periods of kundalini awakening, you are sure to feel at a loss with your sense of self. You might find yourself experiencing a disconnect from everything you have ever known, a strange sense of connection to everything around you, and confusion around your sense of identity. Enduring these experiences may be frightening, but they are all natural to the kundalini awakening and the process of expanding your mind power.

It is safe to say, however, if you are firmly grounded in your perceived self, you are likely going to feel terrified and overwhelmed by the experience of your awakening. During an awakening, there is nowhere you can run to hide from the truth. As it seeps in, you find yourself being caught off guard, forced to shift inner belief systems, and exposed to a world you likely never knew existed. It can be a lot to take in, but it can lead to a phenomenal transformation of self as you discover who you are and what potential you have in this world.

During your kundalini awakening, you will experience complete transformations in your self-orientation. First, you will experience dissolution, and then you will experience substantiation. These are both natural parts of a kundalini awakening, though they can be terrifying as you encounter them because they will completely change your life.

Dissolution of Your Self

Dissolution is the first stage of awakening, as you must willingly accept the breaking down of your present energy field if you welcome in a new plane of existence. As you engage in the dissolution process, you are likely to feel entirely unprepared and terrified about what is going on. Mental confusion, difficulty concentrating, and a tendency to slip back into old behaviors are all natural during the dissolution stage. As you embrace this new version of your identity, you find yourself experiencing sudden, intense fear about what that genuinely means. In order for one variation of yourself to be born, another must die off, which leads to a death and rebirth cycle. Naturally, you may find yourself grieving or clinging to the past, despite knowing that it is time for you to fully embrace the future.

You may find yourself leaning heavily into old coping patterns, only to realize they no longer serve you as they once did. Rather than feeling safe and stable, you feel like you are backsliding, and that creates even more tension and distress. It is essential to avoid these old habits and embrace the next stage of your life if you experience full relief from the past and the discomfort of the dissolution stage.

Those embracing the dissolution stage often feel a strange disconnect from reality, as though they are not genuinely present or there is something blocking them from the moment. You might even find yourself lacking mindfulness about your body and movements, as you begin to physically feel different in the face of change. Clumsiness, discoordination, and mistakes are all more likely to occur during this stage. You may even find yourself experiencing a certain degree of memory loss, a loss of your egoic self, and a disconnect from your sense of self-continuity.

As you embrace all of these terrifying changes, many fascinating things will also come to light. You will become absorbed with signs and symbols and their meanings, as well as the spiritual value of everything around you. With each passing symbol, you find yourself wondering what it means and how it affects your life experience. You might even find yourself intentionally asking for them and then receiving them, which indicates you are more connected than you think, even if you do not presently feel like it.

If you find yourself being overwhelmed by fits of rage, grief, and anxiety, do not fret. These are natural experiences, indicative of you releasing and purging an old sense of reality that no longer serves you or your wellbeing. From here on out, you are on a path of steady momentum, geared directly toward your awakening and the expansion of your mind power. What once was will never be again, and what has yet to come already is.

Substantiation of Your New Self

When you emerge from the dissolution stage, you find yourself embracing substantiation. This allows you to feel how change has affected your life and enjoy the most positive characteristics of an awakening. Once your old self has been purged, and the obsessions and fears associated with it have subsided, you begin to feel peace. Calmness washes over your body as you embrace a more relaxed state, and find all of your cyclical and reactive mental patterns washing away. Blocks are cleared from your mind and energy as you discover a significant sense of personal power and are able to embody it for maximum expansion of your mind power.

Those that reach this stage often find themselves engaged in a clearer and deeper perception of reality, which results in them having less emotional reactions to the world around them. Rather than being hijacked by the primal emotional brain, they are able to see things from a more logical, rational point of view. While they still have emotional experiences and intense ones at that, they are able to observe them from a different perspective and, therefore, the way they experience emotional changes.

Another impressive benefit of reaching the substantiation phase is that you are able to gain more from life itself. With the activation of this higher perception, you become more spontaneous and open to experiencing the world around you. You are no longer phased by judgment, worried about making mistakes, or held back through fear and concern around what might happen. Instead, you embody a higher level of faith and allow yourself to enjoy everything that surrounds you.

Beyond your personal experiences, your interactions with the world around you change, too. Your ability to see through a more rational and peaceful perspective means you can enjoy deeper, more significant relationships with others. When you have awakened, you no longer feel a need to cling to relationships, judge your value based on them, or avoid relationships for fear of being hurt. Instead, you feel comfortable allowing others to enjoy their life, while you also get to enjoy your life. You come together to enrich each other's lives, yet you feel equally as enriched on your own, too. This ability to feel detached from relationships makes it easier for you to genuinely enjoy them, while also showing up more authentically within them, too.

Exploring Life With Your New Identity
Receiving a new identity is empowering, especially if you take the time to explore it and invest in it. Your deepest potential for expanding mind power lies in embodying the entirety of who you are and integrating every aspect into your life. When you can observe, experience, integrate, and embrace, life becomes more enjoyable because you live a life where you genuinely accept all aspects of yourself. In this space, you no longer run away from the parts of

yourself that you dislike or are afraid of. Instead, you accept them and move forward regardless, recognizing that all of these are part of what makes you the dynamic, wonderful individual that you are.

Allowing yourself to embrace this new identity begins with changing the story you have been telling yourself. Even following dissolution and substantiation, you might still be telling yourself outdated stories about who you are and what that means. Your outdated stories no longer feel right, yet they linger because you have yet to fully transform them in your mind. An excellent way to work through this and fully transition the story you are telling yourself is to sit down and journal who you think you are on a deep, core level. Do not journal about who you want to be, how you wish you perceive yourself, or how you "should" perceive yourself. Instead, write down the specific stories you have told yourself about who you are, and what that means. If you are genuinely authentic in this practice, it is likely that the things you write sound harsh and hurt. It's essential to get down these honest, painful explanations; however, as this allows you to release this story about yourself and create a new one that is more accurate.

The next stage of this practice is to adjust the story you are telling about yourself. In other words, write a new one. Again, do not write about who you want to be, how you wish to be, or who you should be. Instead, write about who you are from a positive perspective, and create an identity that feels genuinely connected with who you are. For example, if you previously identified yourself as being flaky, you might now identify yourself as being spontaneous. Or, if you previously identified yourself as being arrogant, you might now identify yourself as being confident. These shifts allow you to observe your exact personality in a new light, which means you can embrace a more optimistic, compassionate, and productive outlook on yourself.

Expanding Your Perception of Self

Your awakening brings about the most rapid, shocking changes; however, you will continue to experience an expansion in your sense of identity as you continually lean into the energies of your awakening. It is essential to avoid clinging to any aspect of your identity, even after your awakening, as doing so can prevent you from allowing further awakening to occur. Realistically, your entire life will be spent evaluating aspects of yourself and letting them fade away so new aspects can emerge. Remaining detached allows you to comfortably release pieces of yourself as they no longer fit so you can embody your new self on a continuous basis.

An excellent way to expand your mind power and embrace your ever-changing self is to regularly engage in a ritual that enables you to see your most recent version of self. Each day, week, or month, spend time writing about who you were and who you are. Keep your story fresh and relevant, and continue to update it as you work through different blocks and cycles of growth. This ensures your perception of self remains authentic and serves you in achieving further growth, as you are no longer holding yourself back with outdated stories. Beyond writing down your new story, be sure to assert it to yourself on a regular basis, so you genuinely believe it, embody it, and experience it in your everyday life.

CHAPTER 10
Using Your Mind As A Problem Solver

The average person uses their mind to process day to day activities, rarely straying away from habit and routine. While there is power in consistency, there is a lack of power when it comes to remaining consistent for a routine you did not intentionally pick, nor create. Far before modern times, man has been succumbing to pre-canned systems that determine how he will live and what he will do with his life. Authority figures have long controlled people by keeping them as a part of the majority, rather than allowing them to become authority figures, often for fear of losing control. These are all excellent resemblances of those that have yet to experience their awakening, as they hold fast to control for fear of losing their grip on others'. Of course, once you are awake, you realize there is no such thing as control, so your focus adverts away from that and toward something far more peaceful and fulfilling.

One of the most empowering journeys you can take following your awakening is the path of problem-solving. Each of our lives is filled with a series of complex issues that drive us to experience various challenges in our everyday lives. It can be easy to remain a victim of these circumstances, especially if you lack awareness around how you can reasonably shift these issues. Fortunately, every problem you face can be solved, and you have the exact power you need to solve those challenges. That power is rooted within your mind and activated through your kundalini awakening.

The Path of Ascended Problem Solving

Prior to their awakening, people often trouble themselves with solving the problems of others or perceiving others as being the root cause of their own problems. Attempting to micromanage others, and blaming others, are two tell-tale signs of a person that has yet to embrace their full awakening. When you approach life from this angle, you are attaching yourself to lower vibrational energy that can actually interrupt the extent of your mind power and sabotage your wellbeing. To fully tap into your awakening and activate your higher powers, you must be willing to embrace a different perspective when addressing problems.

Ascended problem-solving means you no longer look outside of yourself to control or blame others; instead, you look within yourself and seek to deepen your self-control. Your individual problems also shift, as you realize your original concerns were not your genuine concerns. For example, prior to your dissolution, you may have believed your issues were rooted in you being ugly, unlucky, uneducated, or unworthy. Following your awakening, you realize these are not genuine problems and that they never were to begin with. Instead, your likely problems are a lack of self-acceptance, self-appreciation, self-love, and self-motivation. These deeper issues are far more complex and damaging than the issues you previously believed you had.

Beyond seeing the truth behind your troubles, ascended problem solving also allows you to approach it from entirely new energy. Devolved problem solving typically involves you bullying and belittling yourself, and frequently criticizing yourself for things you cannot control. This self-abuse is intended to stimulate change when all it does is make you feel bad about who you are and prevent you from embracing growth. Ascended problem-solving looks like addressing your issues with love and compassion. Rather than abusing yourself for your behaviors, you can witness how your patterns are limiting you and lovingly correct them. Your focus, then, is not on solving problems but supporting your growth.

Achieving ascended problem-solving skills is a practice in itself, as it can be habitual to address your challenges from a self-abusing place. It is essential to approach your problem solving from a grounded, centered place, by focusing on how you can support yourself in having a more positive experience, rather than focusing on how you can prevent yourself from having a negative experience.

Discovering a New Way for Everything

Awakening your ascended problem-solving skills enables you to discover a new way of doing virtually everything in your life. Until now, you have likely been living your life based on other's expectations and what you believed you had to do in order to survive. It can be challenging to realize that nearly every aspect of who you are and what you do, is driven by other people and the expectations they placed on you throughout your life. Recognizing this enables you to intentionally assess each area of your life and design a lifestyle that suits your genuine needs.

Understand that every one of us has unique needs. As you discovered through kundalini and Ayurveda, your energy is unique to you and requires different tools to help you achieve significant balance within yourself. If you desire to achieve full enlightenment, you must become aware of your own energy and intentionally guide it toward a level of balance that serves your expansion. Each aspect of your life, and how you show up for your life, is infused with energy, and your intention allows you to take control over that energy and guide it in a meaningful way.

As you embody intentional energy, avoid rushing to infuse every aspect of your life with it. In doing so, you overwhelm yourself, throw yourself off course, and make it more challenging for you to embrace change. Instead, focus on essential areas of your life first, and allow yourself to expand from there. This way, you experience an intentional change in these key areas, and that change continues to flow out into every area of your life over time. Remember, enlightenment is a journey, not a race, and there is no shame in taking it at your own pace. Walk the path of growth at your own speed, and trust in the process. As long as you listen to your higher soul and trust your energy to guide you, you will find your way to expand mind power.

Becoming the Brightest Version of Yourself

Desiring to be better than everyone else is an egoic wish that naturally fades away as your kundalini energy awakens. There is no difference between yourself and others, nor is there any way to quantify who is better or worse. Finally, there is no reason to quantify such knowledge, as there is no value to being the best or the worst; these are merely ways we attempt to gauge ourselves and create a sense of false pride through our accomplishments. Rather than trying to be better than anyone else, focus on becoming the brightest version of yourself.

It is vital to use terms like "brightest" rather than "best," as describing yourself as being your best self suggests that you also have the worst self, which indicates you have yet to integrate all aspects of yourself. Further, desiring to be your best self means you see yourself as existing in your worst self, and you essentially push yourself away from becoming your best self by always believing that you have yet to get there. By desiring to be your brightest self each day, you embody this bright energy and accept all aspects of yourself as they are. In this, you solve many of your issues simply by accepting who you are and the experiences you have in life.

To become the brightest version of yourself, look for ways to live your day to day life as intentionally as possible. How can you show up authentically? What can you do to enjoy yourself more? Where can you embrace your autonomy? How can you gain more out of each moment? What can you do to support others? Where can you show up more mindfully? Living in alignment with the answers to each of these questions enables you to solve your problems from an ascended perspective and enjoy a higher quality of life. They also support you with expanding your mind power and elevating your kundalini awakening, as you are actively taking charge and embodying the benefits of the awakening itself. As you continue to integrate these benefits into your life, they continue to expand and provide you with greater value.

Expanding Your Power to Others
The devolved self always wants to be better than others, which means it wants to hoard power and avoid sharing anything with anyone else. This is evident in many self-serving authoritative figures; however, it can also be seen in many people existing as a part of the average majority. As you embrace your awakening, you realize that there is no distinction between yourself and others; we are all one. What makes you a human and the experiences you have are the same as what makes me a human, and the experiences I have. While we may have our own personalities, memories, life paths, individual experiences, goals, dreams, relationships, perspectives, and otherwise, at our core essence, we are the same. It is likely that, had I been born into your exact experience, I would have been exactly the same as you are, and you would have also been exactly the same as I am had you been born into mine. At our roots, we are all humans embodying the human experience in one way or another.

Because we are all the same, the way we treat each other heavily affects the way we treat ourselves, too, and vice versa. The way you treat yourself will influence the way you treat others. If you want to become an excellent problem solver and ascend through all of your troubles, it pays to discover how you can assist yourself while also assisting others. Becoming of service to others enables you to better understand their perspectives, educate them on a better way of living, and support them with experiencing more from life.

The key to expanding your power to others is to remain detached from the experience. In other words, serve others when it reflects as a sign of you loving yourself, and never otherwise. When you serve someone else because you genuinely gain joy out of it or because you desire to see the benefit touch their lives, you feel good about helping them. Then, you never feel as though you are being taken advantage of or treated as an unpaid servant. Instead, you feel as though you have shown up for yourself and another at the same time, and you both gain benefit from that.

Remaining detached also means that you do not feel as though you have to micromanage another or force them to receive your support. If someone declines your assistance, you can lovingly accept this and move on. From there on out, you remain detached, so you can allow them to fulfill their own life experience and learn in their own way or not. Because you have granted them the freedom to experience life as they need to, you also grant them the gift of unconditional love and acceptance, which are incredibly valuable to each of us. Plus, when you can unconditionally love and accept another, you can also unconditionally love and accept yourself.

CHAPTER 11
Your Ego Needs Checking

According to the kundalini tradition, the ego must die if you will fulfill your path of enlightenment. The ego is considered the anchor of the unevolved human self, which often serves as a root cause for most suffering. It has been reported that your ego will frequently "flare-up" in an effort to regain control, effectively preventing you from shedding it and living in alignment with truth, rather than ego. The trouble is, your ego has been programmed by society for years and is designed to prevent you from fully stepping into greatness. In most cases, your ego will effectively hold you back and keep you playing small, using emotions such as pride and duty to prevent you from necessary growth and awakening.

As you embody your kundalini awakening, there becomes an inevitable point where your ego must die or, at the very least, be demoted, so it no longer controls you. When you effectively shed your programmed ego, you gain the opportunity to listen carefully to your higher energies and follow the truth, rather than your programming. This concept may seem far-fetched, particularly if you only recently began your awakening experience; however, it is necessary to understand. So long as you continue to allow your ego to run the show, you will succumb to the ego's limitations.

Checking your ego means discovering how to let it naturally fade, to the point of eventual death. The process does not have to be fast, though it can be. It does not have to be painful, though it usually will be. Because you currently lack the ascension that comes from having released your ego, you find yourself struggling to surrender to the process wholly. The ability to surrender as deeply as you need to is often learned and achieved by the time the ego has been fully released. Until then, it is best to embrace the process and trust in the flow, even if the flow sometimes feels painful, challenging, or impossible.

Shedding the Programmed Ego

There are two versions of ego: the programmed ego and the primal ego. The primal ego is something we are all born with, and it is designed to help distinguish the difference between yourself and others. Allowing you to see your individuality means your ego roots you in the present reality, showing you that the human condition includes several individuals taking their own journey to the same place, more or less. This perspective is necessary, as it enables you to see and participate in the same reality everyone else is participating in, which helps connect you to the rest of society.

Over time, your ego is programmed by society. As it continues to shape and identify present reality, your ego evolves to gain a more dynamic understanding of what that actually means. Rather than merely seeing yourself as being separate from everyone else, you now start to formulate stories around what that means and how you can minimize your separateness by adapting to the common values of society. In many cases, these values are not the genuine values of each individual, rather the common values of the unawakened many.

Shedding the programmed ego is the first step of ego death, as it enables you to release pride from aspects of yourself that are not relevant to your well being or your higher life experience. As this aspect of your ego is deprogrammed and released, you gain the ability to see life through a purer set of eyes. In many cases, it feels as though you see the world with childlike wonder because you have released the pain and pressures associated with societal expectations and commands.

The process of shedding your programmed ego will naturally begin when you commence your kundalini awakening. As you continue to awaken, your programmed ego will continue to be shed. In some cases, the shedding will happen as a natural evolution that requires minimal effort on your behalf. Aside from embracing the awakening and embodying the changes, no further effort is required for you to experience the shedding of your programmed ego.

In some cases, however, the shedding process feels more complex than that. When shedding the ego feels more challenging, the best thing you can do is be gentle with yourself and love yourself through the process. Rather than attempting to control, judge, or limit the grief, pain, or distress you are feeling, accept it, and recognize it as being a part of the process. Allow yourself to compassionately and productively feel through and express those emotions, then release them. Once they are gone, you will feel a renewed sense of peace and relief in that part of your existence.

Preventing Your Ego From Holding You Back

As you embrace the ego death process, there will be a deep inner voice demanding you to "go back." This voice will command you to return to safety, avoid your growth, and stop looking crazy. Essentially, it will say everything it feels it needs to in order to prevent you from bravely walking forward and embodying your awakening. This voice *is* your ego, and the many things it is saying reflect your egos desire to remain intact. As far as it is concerned, it is a staple to your wellbeing as it protects you from doing anything wrong and keeps you connected to a greater society. This is precisely the problem, however, as it is keeping you connected in a low vibrational way. You can connect in a higher way if you release the ego itself.

During the death process, you can prevent the ego from holding you back by slipping as deep into surrender as possible. Through surrender, you find trust, and in the trust, you discover the strength; you need to allow the process to take its course so you can be relieved from the pain of your ego. Anytime you find yourself enduring a particularly painful, self-sabotaging, or mentally draining day associated with your ego death, intentionally set aside time to process your feelings. If you can, sit down with your journal and write about what you are feeling and experiencing, and recall what you are looking forward to. As you create this shift within your mind, the emotional aspect of your ego death feels less painful and more endurable. Through it, peace and shift are created.

It is especially important to become aware of your ego, holding you back anytime you actively witness this happening. Part of having a programmed ego is having one that is so sneaky that it behaves subconsciously, without you being aware of what is going on. You can rapidly bring this into your awareness using two techniques: choosing to place your awareness on the behavior of your ego, and observing your life for points of resistance, lack, or struggle. If you experience any of these three things, you can be confident that your ego is running the show in that area of your life.

Drawing your awareness into these behaviors that are typically rooted in your subconscious means you can consciously ascend these behaviors, allowing your ego to die off even more. Once they have been brought into your awareness, complete your journaling process for uncovering them, understanding them, and redirecting yourself toward new, more efficient behaviors. The more consistent you are, the better.

Creating an Egoless Future

The goal of kundalini is to reach a point in your life where you no longer have an ego. The ego death is an ultimate symbolism of enlightenment, as it indicates that you have fully released the lower vibrational elements of being a human. You are now pure enough to enter the kingdom of heaven, so says tradition. Despite the tremendous value of ego death, it is essential to understand that this process does not happen rapidly, nor would you want it to. While it can, and it can even be painless if you manage to fully succumb, most people will not react well to rapid or sudden ego death. Instead, such a rapid death could lead to them experiencing insanity, delusions, or other conditions suffered by those who have had their understanding of reality suddenly torn away from them. To say it is traumatizing would be an understatement.

Continually focusing on your ego death and working toward facilitating it means that, eventually, your entire ego will have died off. Following your natural pace and remaining consistent in your actions means you can look forward to eventually experiencing a total ego death. This may happen in your present lifetime, or it may happen many lifetimes from now when you have had an adequate opportunity to work through all of your karma and release yourself from it.

It is reasonable to understand that not everyone will experience total ego death, nor does everyone want to. For many, their attachment to the human condition keeps them from wanting to experience full ego death, and that is okay. Through kundalini, you can still expand your mind power by shedding the programmed ego in favor of a deprogrammed or primal ego. The unity of a primal ego with a self-aware mind leads to an impressive state of mental expansion, which allows you to tap into the fullness of your personal power.

CHAPTER 12
Happiness Is Your Choice, Make It

Studies have shown that happiness plays an incredible role in your mental health, yet the way you approach happiness may not be serving you. Knowing how to create your own happiness, and live with a lack of happiness, enables you to gain the true value of this beautiful emotion. Further, it allows you to apply an expansive perspective to it and embody the lessons that happiness has to teach you.

Regardless of what anyone says, happiness is a choice that you get to make. Happiness is not linked to your income, appearance, material possessions, perceived personal value, worthiness, or anything else. Happiness is solely linked to your decision to be happy, no matter what.

The Real Path to Happiness

The real path to experiencing genuine happiness is to stop pursuing happiness. As with anything, the more you try to pursue it, the more you reinforce the lack of it in your subconscious mind. Because you are always seeking happiness, your mind concludes that you must presently be without happiness. After all, you would not seek it if you already had it.

Through the lessons of kundalini, you have discovered so much about embodying the energy and embracing all that this energy has to offer you. Applying these same lessons to happiness enables you to tap deeply into the power of your mind and make meaningful choices to your wellbeing. It starts with realizing that happiness is not something you get to; it is something you choose to make and hold within yourself in each individual moment.

Start right now. As you sit here, reading this book, close your eyes and take a few deep breaths into your diaphragm. Then, once you experience the presence of peace in your mind, choose to feel happy in this moment. Continue focusing on the choice of being happy right now until you genuinely feel happy within yourself. Hold onto this decision and continue about your daily life. The real secret to feeling happy is deciding to be happy right now, regardless of what is going on in your life.

How Happiness Improves Your Health

Happiness is not only a spiritual experience; it is also one that improves your wellbeing in a tangible manner. Studies have shown that when you are happy, you are more resilient, have a better immune system, and experience less pain than the average person. Happiness also improves your mental health, supporting you with offsetting depression, anxiety, and other mental health conditions. It can also boost your memory, creativity, and mental clarity.

To create more happiness in your life as a way to boost your health, all you need to do is focus on the things that make you happy right now. Previously, you may have believed that your happiness would be determined by external circumstances beyond your control, or beyond the present moment. Now, you must realize that your happiness can be created right now by things that cost you nothing. Remember a pleasant memory, smell something you like, eat tasty food, have a positive conversation with a friend, say something nice to yourself, or find a reason to laugh in the moment. These are all excellent ways to make yourself happy in the moment, so you can experience the benefits of success right away, regardless of what is going on in your life.

Consciously Choosing to Be Happy

As with anything, consciously choosing to be happy in each moment requires practice. It takes a significant amount of energy to increase your conscious awareness, let alone with the intention of monitoring and adjusting your day to day life. If you wish to consciously choose to be happy, you must not only expand your conscious awareness but discover how to use it to adjust your behavior.

To expand your conscious awareness, you must simply become knowledgeable in controlling your awareness filter. This filter is attuned to recognize anything you ask it to, and it is incredibly efficient with its job. Think about it, before you bought the current car you drive, it is likely that this specific model of car did not stand out to you on the road. Once you started thinking about buying it, and after you acquired it, you started seeing it everywhere. Why? Because it has been brought into your conscious awareness as a substantial piece of information. This is a prime example of your awareness filter.

Expanding your consciousness starts with adjusting your awareness filter to look for areas of opportunity. Do this by recognizing your symptoms of happiness and setting your awareness filter to look for signs of happiness. Then, go through your normal daily experience and observe how your awareness filter automatically draws your attention to your symptoms of happiness. This is an excellent sign, as it means you are fully capable of becoming aware of anything you desire, based on what you request from your filter.

Now that you can comfortably observe periods of happiness, see if you can adjust your filter to become aware of times when you are not happy. Perhaps there are specific points in your day when you can benefit from happiness, yet you are not yet making the decision to feel that way. Recognize the symptoms that indicate that you have arrived at that point, then draw your awareness filter to this part of yourself. Anytime you observe these choice points in action, use your breath (Prana) and the power of choice to embody happiness, even if happiness seems like the most challenging decision to make in that moment.

Continue making the conscious decision to bring happiness into your life. As often as you can, observe areas where you would benefit from greater happiness and make a choice to create happiness in that space. If you cannot invoke happiness through a simple breath, consider ways you can adjust those areas of your life to set yourself up for happiness in advance. This way, you intentionally create a more positive experience, rather than allowing yourself to continually fall victim to unhelpful patterns.

Embracing a Lack of Happiness

Happiness is not a lifelong emotion. No emotions are. Each emotion you feel is fleeting and ends sooner than you likely think it will. Increasing your awareness around this ensures that, as you experience emotions, you also experience detachment from them. This way, you allow them to live out their natural course and provide yourself with an abundance of space to feel and experience life in its entirety.

Acknowledging that happiness is among one of the many temporary emotions you experience means you accept that there will be periods in your life that lack happiness altogether. When you are grieving, experiencing pain, or suffering for any reason, for example, you may feel an absence of happiness in your life. This does not imply that you cannot look for reasons to be optimistic, but it does mean that you are unlikely to experience genuine happiness in that moment. At times, you may be comfortable in that lack of happiness and unwilling to do anything to change it, which is acceptable, healthy, and normal.

When you experience a lack of happiness in your life, it is essential that you do not make any judgments around this. Avoid judging your emotions, your preferences, or the way you navigate that life experience. Instead, embrace it, accept it, and consider your chosen approach as being the one you need to embody the experience of "being okay." Being okay is achievable in any state, so long as we are open to accepting the emotions we are feeling.

Should you ever feel troubled by your lack of happiness, recall that happiness always comes back, just as sadness always ends. The sooner you surrender to your emotions, the sooner you can express them and heal through them as you return to a more positive, pleasant state. It is perfectly reasonable to understand that experiencing a lack of happiness means that the return of your happiness is far more gratifying, as it provides you with a renewed appreciation for the feeling itself. Be patient, compassionate, and loving toward yourself, and all will pass, soon.

CHAPTER 13
How You Treat Them Is How You Treat You

A beautiful concept that the average human frequently fails to recognize is that the way you treat others equates to the way you treat yourself, and vice versa. Generally speaking, if you have a positive, wholesome relationship with yourself, you will have an easier ability to have a positive and wholesome relationship with others, too. If you wish to experience more love, compassion, empathy, reliability, permanency, or anything else in your relationships with other people, you must embrace that in your relationship with yourself. Further, if you wish to see and experience the best in humanity, you must see and experience the best within yourself. Expanding the quality of your relationship with yourself directly expands the quality of your relationship with others, allowing you to gain greater fulfillment from life.

Why Your Intrapersonal Relationship Matters

They say that in order for someone else to love you, you must first love yourself. This is an ineffective way of getting the point across, as the more accurate message is that the more you love yourself, the more you can observe and receive love from others'. How much you love yourself holds zero impact on others' capacity to love you, but one hundred percent impact on your capacity to accept that love from others'.

We all desire high-quality relationships filled with mutual love, respect, compassion, acceptance, understanding, and growth. To embody that with someone else provides us with the opportunity to experience the highest potential in our relationships, which we believe will make us feel better. Once again, there is a delusional belief here. Those who have yet to awaken will likely believe that the improved feelings come from the higher-quality relationships with others when it actually comes from the quality of the relationship we have with ourselves in order to facilitate those improved relationships.

Simply put, you cannot engage in these high-quality relationships if you are not first in a place with yourself where you can reasonably show up to these relationships in a healthy manner. If you bring in limiting patterns or behaviors, you are introducing sabotage to your relationships and limiting the extent to which you can receive from them. You must learn to fully detach from your relationships to gain the most out of them, and to achieve this detachment; you must have a strong enough relationship within yourself to feel safe doing so. If you lack that strong connection to yourself, releasing your connection from others' feels impossible because these relationships are fulfilling needs, you believe you cannot fulfill yourself. The trouble is, your inability to fulfill them yourself means you settle for anyone willing to try, and you are always landing in unhealthy relationships with unhelpful expectations since you are asking people for something they genuinely cannot offer.

Becoming your own rock means you can independently fulfill your needs, which makes your relationships more supplemental than anything. Yes, they maintain a necessary value in your life; however, you no longer need to attach to them to suck as much energy out of them as possible. Instead, you can allow people to be themselves and enjoy their own life experiences without having to demand their time, attention, or change, because you, too, can enjoy your own life experience in your own way. This autonomy and respect create space for high quality, healthy relationships to exist between yourself and others.

Expanding the Quality of Your Relationship to Self

Fixating on how to improve your relationships with others is the wrong approach to take when it comes to creating a positive link between how you treat yourself and others. So long as you continue to focus on external relationships as a way to facilitate these improvements, you will continue to experience limitations as you wait on other people to behave the way you need them to for you to change. Practically speaking, this is an ineffective approach to improving your relationships.

A more appropriate and effective approach is to improve your relationship with yourself, which will naturally improve your relationship with others. Further, it will welcome more people into your life that are a better fit for you, which will make enjoying enriching and meaningful relationships more accessible. How you improve your relationship with yourself entirely depends on what your present relationship looks like. Though there are plenty of excellent steps you can take to get started.

One excellent way to develop a positive relationship with yourself is to express gratitude for yourself and your body, especially. Being grateful for the body you have and the experiences you create is a wonderful way to develop a closer connection with yourself. You should also be kind to yourself, including your mind, emotions, body, and spirituality. Say empowering things to yourself, take care of yourself, and engage in practical measures to support your wellbeing from a physical vantage point. In kundalini, physical activities are fundamental because people have long known that your body matters to your wellbeing. If you desire to achieve greater enlightenment, you must have the healthiest body you can to get there. The purer your body, the purer your energy and the more aligned your field will be.

It also pays to release your inner perfectionist and judgment. Attempting to be perfect at everything effectively keeps you from pursuing anything, for fear of enduring the messy beginner stages or the mistakes that come with increasing your skill in any area of your life. Your judgment feeds your perfectionism but also serves to sabotage you in many other ways, as well. For example, your judgment increases separation between yourself and others, damages your relationship with people you care about, harms your relationship to yourself, and positions you as a bully in many people's stories. Judgment does nothing to aid your wellbeing, only to hinder it. If you want to improve your relationship with yourself, you must cut judgment out completely.

Lastly, you need to notice and redirect your inner critic. Your inner voice is often powered by your ego and serves to protect you by invoking fear and other limiting emotions that prevent you from faithfully pursuing your destined path. As you shed your programmed ego and work toward developing a positive relationship with yourself, you must become observant of your inner voice and correct it whenever you need to. Always redirect it toward more loving, fulfilling, and nurturing voices, so it supports you. The more empowering you are toward yourself, the stronger your relationship with yourself will be.

Unconditional Love and Acceptance of Others

Expanding your relationship with yourself will inevitably expand your love and acceptance of others. As you witness the complexities of self-love and come to understand the impact of your experience, you will discover it is far easier for you to accept others that are also struggling with this path. Your heightened awareness from your awakening also provides you with the opportunity to lovingly accept anyone that has not yet chosen or is actively resisting the path of awakening themselves to their full energy. In fact, this is essential as it not only increases the quality of your relationships but also dramatically expands your mind power.

As you release your need to worry about others and how they are behaving or the way they are affecting you, you increase your expendable mental space. Now that you no longer have to monitor and manage everyone else, you can focus on deepening your self-awareness and monitoring and managing yourself. Here, you can use this level of awareness to expand your relationship to yourself, while also allowing that to expand the quality of your relationship to others.

A wonderful way to begin expressing unconditional love and acceptance toward others also happens to be an excellent tool for times when expressing these unconditional emotions seems challenging or even impossible. At times, particularly when you are upset by the way someone else is behaving, it is necessary to take additional action toward releasing feelings of resistance and opening up to feelings of unconditional love and acceptance.

The tool best used is called loving kindness meditation. This meditation is used to express love and acceptance to people, especially those we are troubled by, so we can dissolve our resistance and increase our own good vibes. Kundalini especially embraces this, encouraging you to release others' from your mind so you can address your own karma while they address theirs.

To engage in a loving kindness meditation, start by relaxing and engaging in meditative breath. When you have reached a point where you feel calm and centered, you can begin expressing loving kindness to anyone and anything that crosses your mind. Continue expressing it until you genuinely feel a sense of love and kindness toward that person or thing. An excellent way to invoke this is to simply repeat, "I love you and accept you unconditionally," which draws your focus and encourages you to embody these feelings. You may have to do multiple sessions for particularly stubborn experiences; however, you will begin to embody significantly higher levels of love and acceptance toward others through this repeated practice.

Empowering All From Your Expanded Awareness

Ascending into a higher relationship with yourself and others means exploring how you can lovingly empower yourself and others from this new state of awareness. One significantly meaningful way of empowering others, and yourself, is to hold space for everyone to be who they genuinely are. People each have their own unique qualities, strengths, attractive features, weaknesses, and ugliness. No one is exempt from experiencing both the positive and negative aspects of being a human, not even yourself. Rather than holding unreasonable expectations that everyone abandons their weaknesses and ugly sides in favor of their strengths and attractive sides, it is more meaningful to hold space for people to simply be. This way, you and all who surround you do not feel pressured to hide their ugliness and flaws from the world around them.

In holding space for others, be willing to forgive their mistakes and continue to love and accept them unconditionally, even if they have messed up. Hold that same level of forgiveness for yourself, too. Believe in everyone's ability to be a better person, and do what you can to uplift people so they can witness that in themselves, too. Do not punish yourself, or them, if it fails. Instead, lovingly accept where they are at, and that you are incapable of forcing anyone to do anything, at any time. Whenever you see someone genuinely exert effort into something, praise them and celebrate their wins. Even if their wins are small, or they themselves cannot see the value of those wins, celebrate them. Celebrate yourself abundantly, too.

As you continue to uplift and empower others through your unconditional desire to support, love, and accept, you will witness the quality of your relationships to yourself and others growing. Through this, you experience greater mind power and an expanded ability to enjoy all that life has to offer.

CHAPTER 14
Becoming Your Biggest Cheerleader

Kundalini *is* a journey to self-empowerment. Yes, it enables you to improve the quality of your relationships with others and the experiences you have with the world around you, but the number one purpose is to improve everything for yourself. By embodying this level of selfishness, you provide yourself with the ability to become your own biggest cheerleader. Through that, you naturally show up in a more meaningful way for the world around you, too.

Feeling the Entirety of Your Presence

Awakening your kundalini means you are exposed to the dynamic energies that make up every aspect of who you are, from your body to your soul, and even your connection to god. Your ability to cheer yourself on is amplified when you realize your presence is far greater than a mere body with a persistent voice living in its head. Grasping the entirety of who you are means recognizing that there is so much more of you to cheer on, and so much more of you cheering when you do. It is no longer just you and your history of life experiences and external influences. Now, it is you, your higher self, your god-self, and the presence of your god themselves. Your team is vast and entirely rooted within yourself.

Upon awakening and activating these energies, you realize that life is much bigger than you may have previously realized. The vastness of life itself means that everything is worth celebrating, including you. Further, you realize you are deeply supported in being yourself and celebrating the experience of showing up as this brilliant individual. Rather than looking to others for validation, love, and acceptance, you can comfortably look toward yourself and confidently receive all of these and more.

As you engage in your daily meditation sessions, welcome in the entirety of your presence both earthly and beyond. Use your breath to invoke life force energy and feel the connection between yourself and the divine, and allow that connection to empower you. Through this, you will find many reasons to celebrate.

Celebrating Yourself on Every Level

The unawakened individual celebrates only the tangible wins they experience, particularly those that can earn them status. For example, they happily celebrate career promotions, engagements, new homes, children, and other such status symbols. However, they rarely celebrate the seemingly lesser things that carry just as much, if not more of an impact on their overall growth. For example, they fail to celebrate their smaller actions taken toward achieving their goals, such as the daily tasks they complete to get them closer to their win.

Learning to celebrate everything about yourself, right down to the smallest details of your physical, mental, emotional, and spiritual growth is invaluable to your success. As you celebrate yourself, you actively become your own biggest cheerleader. In that, you uncover an abundance of joys in life, each of which enriches your experience. For example, you find happiness, fulfillment, self-trust, self-confidence, a positive relationship with yourself, and a desire to continue doing more as you move into greater levels of expansion.

Embracing Fearlessness In Your Life

Fear is a natural, functional element of life. You experience fear because your body is wired to. Under necessary circumstances, fear provides you with the adrenaline rush required to fight or flight, allowing you to save your life from a wild tiger or a hungry bear. In modern circumstances, there are few situations where you need fear to come into play. However, you must discover how to relieve yourself of fear because it will inevitably make its way into your life anyway.

One of the fastest ways to embrace fearlessness in your life is to recognize that you have a significant energy source behind you. As you breathe in, you invoke life force energy in your very body. This unites you to your entire self, as well as the gods above. Through this, you have all the power you need to persevere through any challenge you face, no matter how significant.

Calling on this greater power to support you through life does not invoke total fearlessness, but it will drastically downplay the fear you experience while expanding your faith. This combination empowers you to move through any obstacle, as you feel as though you have a genuine reason to celebrate and cheer yourself on.

Living as Your Authentic Self

Lastly, you need to live as your authentic self. The value of a cheerleader is that they cheer you on to becoming your best, and becoming your best means living as your most authentic self. Despite you having the same essence as everyone else on earth, you are made up in a unique manner and express in a way that is different from anyone else. The offering you have for earth and other humans is also unique to you, and can only be achieved when you clear out your limitations and live in alignment with your authentic self.

As your inner cheerleader cheers you on and encourages you to embrace higher levels of being, you must oblige and embody those very energies. The more you do, the more you reinforce that you are capable and worthy of embracing these higher aspects of yourself. You also reinforce your cheerleader by following through and validating his or her power and presence in your life. Moreover, when you live as your authentic self, your inner cheerleader has more reasons to shout, "YES!"

Each of us needs a healthy dose of convincing from time to time, especially if we genuinely believe that the activity we are about to make could harm us in some way, even if only through a minor inconvenience. Embracing your inner cheerleader, playing deeply into the role, and following through on the actions your cheerleader motivates you to take are all essential ways to become the brightest version of yourself through meaningful acts of self-motivation.

CHAPTER 15
Love Conquers All... Really

At the core of expanding your mind power lies one phenomenal energy that you must embody if you wish to achieve anything. That is, love.

Love provides you with the necessary energy to move through anything, no matter how challenging or overwhelming it may be. Through love, you can ascend judgment, hate, pain, and virtually every other circumstance you are faced with. Where love exists, no negative feelings can, because there is a deep core desire to experience connection, fulfillment, and positivity in spite of anything else you might face.

In kundalini, unconditional love is said to be the way to ascension and a powerful way to overcome the limitations of the ego. Through the presence of love, you gain the capacity to move beyond attachments that keep you rooted in pain and welcome the energy of growth and positivity instead. If you wish to experience the greatness of life, you must first move into the light of love. There, you find the freedom to ascend at your own pace and in your own way.

Love to Overcome Ego

Love is a potent antidote to ego. As you continue on your journey of overcoming the programmed ego and embracing the primal ego, or ego death, you can embody love as a powerful tool. Through love, you accept all aspects of self, including that which you like and that which you do not. You dissolve all attachments to aspects of yourself that you like or dislike most, meaning you are free to move between identities and embrace an ever-expanding version of yourself.

Instead of becoming attached to the process of your ego deprogramming or death, discover how you can love yourself and your ego. Unconditionally love the value it brought you in the past, and love yourself for any challenges you faced as a direct result of your ego. Come to understand that your ego is not bad nor evil. It is merely an experience you have had that you are now willing to release in favor of feeling your best and enjoying the unconditional growth that comes with letting it go.

Unconditional Love Is the Goal

Unconditional love is, by far, the biggest goal of kundalini. This is the energy gifted to us by the heavens, and the energy we will return to when we ascend from our life experiences. Learning to embrace it in your everyday life allows you to dissolve the attachment, ascend your awareness, and live the truth in a more grounded, practical manner.

This energy also allows you to embrace the true power of your mind by erasing limiting attachments, expanding your heart toward growth, and giving you the faith and confidence you need to try new things. As you continue to expand into these new experiences and adventures, you discover more, your understanding of life deepens, and you tap into greater levels of power held within your mind.

The process of tapping into unconditional love requires you to call on the forces of your mind by sitting back and observing the many values you gain from everything in your life, even the more troubling experiences that you tend not to enjoy as much. As you begin to uncover the value of everything, whether you enjoy it or not, you realize that your life is made for you, and there is always a purpose behind everything you experience. Thus, it becomes easier to embrace everything through unconditional love, and use that love to tap into the abundance of lessons that life has to offer you.

The Eightfold Theory of Love

In kundalini, there is an eightfold theory of love, which introduces why unconditional love is so valuable in the first place. By studying the theory of love and why we require it in our lives, you expand your awareness around this empowering energy and uncover ways to embrace it in your everyday life.

The first aspect of the theory of love is the theory itself. The theory of love and hate is a simple one, outlining that we all desire to love and experience love, yet we go through phases where we are unable to maintain the flow of love, which leads to a variety of emotions, often ending in hate. From hate, we experience vengeance, and through vengeance, we reach destruction, which is where we begin to cause unnecessary chaos in our lives and the lives of others. Everything starts with love, as love is the basic law of life.

The second aspect of the theory of love is called hook and hooker, which is a game involving two or more individuals. This game is often played as a way of establishing security, which is only an illusion. In this case, one person desires to attract the love of others, and the others desire to love that individual. Through this, there seems to be a balance in love, yet there is not one. Unless all can love each other unconditionally, it is a game that no one will win.

The third aspect of the theory of love is that emotional love is not the same as unconditional love. With emotional love, you feel fulfillment in others' and reject your personal reality, making it inferior to others. In this case, you may behave like a caregiver or to value everyone else's happiness above your own, effectively sabotaging your experience with love.

The fourth aspect of the theory of love is commotional love. This is a love that interlocks with emotional fantasy and uses the ego to create habits of insecurity and attitudes with bad manners. When you engage in commotional love, you experience hollowness, shallowness, a lack of fulfillment, inferiority, anger, fear, trauma, impotency, and sleepless nights. Rather than embracing true unconditional love, you have attached yourself to a chaotic form of love that is not beneficial to anyone.

The fifth aspect of the theory of love is circumstantial love. This form of love is produced by the pressure of time and space and has the capacity to change with time and space, too. When you embody circumstantial love, you fail to embrace unconditional love because you are conditioned by the circumstances themselves.

The sixth aspect of the theory of love is real love. Real love enables you to promote, serve, and invest in another's excellence while still embodying and embracing your own excellence. Through this experience of love, you feel another's soul and understand them in a way that is deeper than you can achieve with any other form of love.

The seventh aspect of the theory of love is self-love, which accounts for an understanding of your own existence and the love you have for yourself. At the root of all that you achieve in life is self-love, which drives you to experience the freedom to engage in selflessness and unconditional love with others. This type of love is deeply fulfilling and expansive and paves the way for an entirely new experience in love.

The eighth aspect of the theory of love is infinite love, which is the love you experience when you tap into the energy of your infinite wisdom and reality. This love is often achieved once you have awakened and balanced your crown chakra, which is responsible for your connection to the divine. A wholesome connection here leads to an empowering ability to expand the infinite aspects of your love for others.

CHAPTER 16
Set Goals And Accomplish Them, Often

Setting goals is a tremendous way to motivate yourself to experience more in life and creates a brilliant opportunity to expand the power of your mind. The human mind craves to be challenged, and providing it with goals complete with obstacles is an excellent way to challenge yourself to achieve more. Through the introduction of kundalini, your approach for creating and achieving goals will transform as you embrace a new way of ascending through the many challenges of life. You still must set goals and aspire to achieve them; however, the specific goals you set and the way they have achieved changes entirely. From your heightened awareness and perspective, you realize that there are greater ways to achieve success and to pursue success that is more meaningful to you overall.

The Achieve and Integrate Cycle

Those that have yet to awaken frequently approach their goals with a steadfast desire to push through no matter what and force their way to the end. Often, they reach the end of their goals, feeling a momentary sense of happiness, followed by a deep need to pursue something else. Over time, their achievements stack, yet their sense of victory fails to stack, so they often reach a point of success accompanied by a feeling of hollowness or emptiness.

As you approach your goals from an ascended position, you embrace a cycle of growth that is associated with achieving and integrating. Essentially, this means you work toward fulfilling your goals in life while frequently pausing to allow yourself to integrate each new phase of achieving your goals. Further, you do not push toward fulfilling your goals; you attract the necessary steps to fulfill them and enable yourself to remain focused by receiving intuitive guidance and following the path of least resistance. You must still address challenges, face hardships, and overcome obstacles; however, you experience a more significant level of faith in yourself and your destiny, which allows you to follow the path confidently. Through this, you truly embrace the path of least resistance, allowing you to achieve greater heights of success in virtually every area of your life.

Setting Goals for Your Ascended Self

Setting goals for your ascended self is unlike setting goals for your pre-awakened self. Prior to your awakening, you likely fixated on goals that were associated with your status, appearance, and material gains. You might have desired a slimmer body, larger muscles, a bigger or newer house, a fancier car, a better wardrobe, or any other number of things that would have made you appear better in the eyes of others. While desiring for these things is not inherently bad, it often takes away from your ability to recognize what you truly desire.

Setting goals for your ascended self should be less focused on the external world and your status and power over others, or their opinion of you, and more focused on yourself and what you want to experience in life. This may involve the external world; however, it should be largely focused on your internal self and experiences. Goals relating to how you can experience more from life, gain more joy from each moment and deepen your mindfulness are far more impressive and impactful than goals surrounding your status or worldly achievements. Further, they bring greater levels of fulfillment and significant satisfaction when you do achieve them.

The most effective way to set these ascended goals is to ask yourself: "How do I genuinely want to feel?" Then write the answer down. Your answer to this question defines what your ascended goals should be.

Reaching the Goals Energetically

Reaching goals energetically is as important as reaching them practically. Practical goal-reaching enables you to tick that goal off your list, but if you have not embodied that goal on a deep level, it seems as though you have accomplished nothing. Rather than feeling accomplished and fulfilled, you are left feeling as though your accomplishment was not a big deal, or was not as meaningful as you hoped it would be. Through energetic investment, your goals become more meaningful, and you are able to fully embody the joy of having reached them.

Investing energetically in your goals also enables you to reach them faster. When you experience full-bodied investment in the things that matter to you, you make power moves. Rather than sitting by passively waiting for things to turn in your favor, you invest fully into making them happen. This is the energy people get into when they rapidly shift their lives and manifest their deepest desires. Through this energy, you can have a significant impact on your wellbeing. It is well worth it for you to embrace this level of energy if you want to have a massive impact on your life, and tap into the entirety of your mind power.

Embodying Your Accomplishments

Lastly, you must embody your accomplishments. There is no sense in pursuing a meaningful goal, only to let it slip and fall back to negative patterns after you have reached it. Since your goals are no longer associated with your material gains, it is more essential than ever that you invest in seeing those goals through and embodying them full-time. Creating meaningful habits around your goals is an excellent way to turn them into embodied changes, which allows you to gain the most from them.

The other benefit of embodying your accomplishments is the value it gives your mind. Practically speaking, each time you reach a goal and celebrate that win, your brain experiences a rush of dopamine that is released to reward you for your success. This dopamine rush provides you with the encouragement you need to continually pursue more of your goals, and achieve more significant accomplishments.

A powerful way to fully embody your accomplishments is to affirm your success to yourself and genuinely celebrate yourself for the win. Consider yourself as successful as you would an Olympian that just won their first gold medal, and celebrate yourself with as much gusto and intention as you would celebrate that individual, even if your win seems significantly smaller. That level of self-recognition and self-celebration encourages you to witness the value of your win, and continually work toward embodying further gains, too. Through this, you create a meaningful way to expand your mind power and embody the entirety of who you are through each new stage of your life.

CHAPTER 17
Create Healthy Habits

Habits are a practical aspect of life, are natural to your biology, and hold significant impact over your capacity to expand and reach into the depths of your mind power. From a biological and primal perspective, habits enable you to remove the conscious thought from routine experiences so you can conserve energy and invest it elsewhere. For example, if you always wake up, go to the bathroom, then start a pot of coffee, this becomes a habit, so your brain no longer has to invest energy into running your conscious mind through this loop. Instead, you simply do it on "autopilot."

Everything in our lives has been linked to one habit or another, unless you are particularly spontaneous in which case you still experience many things from a conscious perspective. Regardless of how spontaneous you may be, though, you will always find yourself engaging in a variety of habits, some of which benefit your life, and others that don't.

Creating healthy habits is a wonderful way to reinforce your sense of wellbeing, while also expanding space in your life for you to enjoy greater mind power. You can integrate healthy habits into your life by first understanding the habit loop, then understanding the essential tool of the habit pivot.

The habit loop was defined by psychologists as being a four-step cycle that reinforces itself, effectively wiring your brain with seemingly essential habits. The four steps are this: trigger, routine, reward, reinforce. Each time you experience these four steps, the habit becomes stronger and more deeply instilled in your mind. To break or change your habit, you must know how to use a habit pivot. The pivot means that your trigger, reward, and reinforcement stay the same, but your action changes. This is an essential piece of knowledge that allows you to quickly change any habit you engage in, effectively creating freedom from actions that cause issues in your life. For example, if you presently smoke, your trigger may be stress, smoking is the action, the reward is the freedom from stress, and the reinforcement is the dopamine rush you gained from following through. To pivot this habit, you will maintain your trigger (stress), your reward (relief from stress), and your reinforcement (the dopamine rush), but you will need to pivot your actions. You might pivot to chewing gum, running, or engaging in any other activity that allows you to eliminate stress. In doing so, you transform your habits using the path of least resistance.

Physically Embodying Healthy Habits

The power of your mind, and your capacity to live with activated kundalini energy, rely on you having a strong, healthy body. Embodying healthy habits like eating nutritional meals, staying hydrated, moving your body, sleeping properly, and taking care of any health considerations unique to you is important. Each person requires a different regimen as far as physical health goes, so it is valuable to spend time exploring your body, understanding your needs, and investing in creating a routine that works for you.

Though your physical wellness routine, and corresponding habits, may seem largely practical and even removed from your spiritual experience, you must realize the importance they carry with your spiritual well being. Without a sound body, you are unable to fully ground the power of spirit within you, as there is weakness and stress throughout your system. This does not mean you have to be free of illness; plenty of people live with illness and have a sound body that is capable of embodying the energy of spirit. You must uncover what wellness means for you and your unique body, and strive to live in the healthiest way possible. Do the things that allow your body to be at its strongest and thrive in its own way.

It can be easy to slip on habits that support our physical wellness, because the body is resilient. Despite not being adequately cared for, your body can still move you through many obstacles and allow you to achieve many things in life. You must never settle for a body that merely gets by, though. Create habits that allow your body to thrive, as this is the highest level of respect you can show yourself.

Healthy Habits for Your Limitless Mind

Like with physical habits, it can be easy to let your mental habits slip. Regardless of your wellness plan, your mind will run and will bring you forward through life. It can be easy to succumb to negativity bias, complaining, and complacency when you do not take adequate care of your mind. Many also find it easy to fall into victim patterns, people pleasing, and complete burnout because they engage in habits that are not healthy to their mind.

To tap into your limitless mind power and fully embody the power of life force energy, you must learn to take proper care of your mind. Healthy habits that nourish your mind involve stress-relieving habits, reading, pursuing personal growth, learning, engaging in puzzles, reinforcing your memory, and engaging in optimistic and positive thinking. The more you allow yourself to tap into the expansive capabilities of your mind and use them to your advantage, especially with problem-solving and gaining the most out of life, the stronger your mindset habits will be. Through this, you drastically improve your mind power.

Caring for Your Emotions With Healthy Habits

Your emotions tie into your mental habits, though they stand alone. While mental behaviors include things like self-talk, memory, and problem-solving, emotional behaviors include the actual creation, expression, and release of your emotions. Healthy emotional habits are designed to support your ability to intentionally choose your emotions, express them in a meaningful way, and release them when you are done with them. This expands your mind power by providing you with direct control over your emotional self and the ability to use your emotions to your advantage. Rather than being hijacked by your emotions, which is common when your primal brain takes control, you learn how to stimulate them and use them to your advantage. Emotions will still be spontaneously created through uncontrollable day to day experiences; however, you will have a significant advantage with navigating and expressing your emotions intentionally. You may also use them to impact intentional, meaningful change in your life.

Excellent habits involving emotional health include spending time investing in the creation of emotions you desire, developing self-awareness around your emotional experiences, and creating space for you to express and release your emotions intentionally. This is especially important if you frequently find yourself experiencing emotions at times where it may be inappropriate to express such emotions. Providing yourself adequate time to bring them back to the surface and work through them later is an excellent way to fully release them, so they no longer sit in your energy field, sabotaging your mind power and embodiment of spiritual energy.

Nurturing Your Spirit With Healthy Habits

Although your spirit is an intangible aspect of yourself, it plays a large role in your wellbeing. Embodying healthy habits that nurture your spirit is an empowering way to elevate the quality of your life. Many people neglect their spiritual well being entirely, largely based on the fact that they cannot see, touch, or experience their spirit in a tangible manner. This unfortunate approach leads to feelings of disconnect, isolation, and a lack of faith, which can significantly damage your self-confidence and self-esteem.

Creating healthy habits that nurture your spiritual well being enables you to experience the support, faith, and growth that come from being deeply connected. Excellent spiritual habits include reinforcing your faith, praying, meditating, connecting with your energy, calling on your energy, and relying on the guidance you receive. You also support your spiritual wellbeing and connection each time you take care of your physical, mental, and emotional wellbeing, as you create a sound foundation for your spiritual self to exist.

CHAPTER 18
Open Yourself Up To Change

Change is a beautiful, necessary aspect of life. Our modern perception of change is often delusional and even damaged. We see change as a necessity for economic growth or increased power, often using it as a tool to feed our ego and our materialistic gains. Our view of change implies we must always be in control of change and leading the changes in our lives head on. The idea of releasing control and allowing change to happen seems unnatural, illogical, and even risky as we fear that doing so could lead to us experiencing change in a negative way. Of course, change is inevitable and, despite our best efforts, is rarely housed within our control. Yes, you may influence the change in your life, yet you cannot directly control it. Adjusting your perspective of change, and opening yourself to the natural evolution of life, is necessary to your wellbeing and the embodiment of your mind power.

Embodying a Daily Kundalini Ritual

Kundalini is a powerful catalyst, aiding you in transforming everything in your life from the inside out. Embodying a daily kundalini ritual enables you to invoke, embody, and engage in the power of life force energy. As you work through your ritual, you invite in the energies that motivate transformation and inspire change in your life. Further, the actual embodiment of a daily kundalini ritual will likely be a change in and of itself, because you are now creating from a space of intention and energy.

Each time you engage in your kundalini ritual, make space for you to set an intention and use that intention to your advantage. Call in the guidance of your intuition, life force energy, and the gods and heavens to support you with navigating change, whether it be specific or in general. Allow yourself to embody that guidance and follow it faithfully, as it moves you through any changes you may face in a fluid, comfortable manner.

Opening Yourself Up to Change

Despite change being a necessary and inevitable part of life, you may struggle with the concept of change. Perhaps you are afraid of opening up to change, for fear of losing the comfort you have created for yourself. As humans, we equate comfort to safety, which means we have no need to fear our stability. In other words, we have no need to fear our ability to survive because we have secured our survival through safety and comfort. The idea of expanding beyond your comfort zone and embracing change is terrifying, as it means moving away from the safety and putting yourself "at risk."

Fortunately, our modern lives are rarely risky to the point of your survival being threatened, and the steps you take to expand beyond your comfort zone are unlikely to threaten you, either. By adjusting your perspective and realizing that change is valuable and meaningful, you create space for positive change to occur in your life.

An excellent perspective to embody when it comes to addressing change is the perspective of detached evolution. The idea that we can stay fixed in our comfort zones and remain comfortable, prevent change, or control change, leads to stress when we realize that change is inevitable and rarely controllable. Through the perspective of detached evolution, you release the need for everything to go your way, or for things to turn out as you plan them to. Instead, you lean into faith and trust everything to turn out positively, or at least in a way that you can adapt to.

Work With Change Intentionally

Despite the fact that you cannot control change, there are many things you can control within change itself. You can cause change, embrace change, and work with the natural flow of change to influence it to go your way. Though you may not be able to stimulate the exact changes you desire, you can encourage the outcome to be more favorable or closer to your preferences. Often, the result of change will always be something far more meaningful than what you originally intended anyway, as change is life's natural way of moving us through our earthly experiences.

Working with change intentionally can be done at three separate stages: the cause of change, the behavior of change, and the outcome of change. You may cause change by identifying areas in your life where change must occur and behaving differently in these areas. Showing up with different energy, attitude, and actions can motivate these areas of your life to be transformed entirely. It may take a while for change to sink in; however, the more you embody these changed behaviors within yourself, the greater the catalyst will become for the change you are affecting.

During the behavior of change, you may identify the changes that are occurring and work within them to influence them to work to your benefit. For example, let's say you are moving to a new house in a new city, which is a change you caused. You may not be able to control who you meet, what types of friendships you have, or how you fit into your new community; however, you can take action to encourage this to be a positive experience. By working in alignment with change, you keep yourself open to meeting the right people that add value to your life and support you with feeling a sense of belonging in your new community.

When you reach the outcome of change, you may work with it intentionally by accepting the outcome and discovering ways that you can use the outcome to your advantage. Perhaps it did not turn out as you expected, or it even turned out poorly. You can always pick up the pieces, adapt to the outcome, or effect further change if you are displeased with the way things turned out. Through these actions, you gain the ability to work in harmony with change, rather than push against it or live with a lack of peace due to your ever evolving circumstances.

Being the Most Adaptable Version of Yourself

Embracing change is easiest if you become the most adaptable version of yourself. Being adaptable means that, regardless of what happens in your life, you can adapt and experience the highest quality of life possible. This is a deeply peaceful space to exist in, as it enables you to embrace all aspects of life without pushing against them or clinging for things to stay the same.

Mindset is your most powerful weapon in adaptability, as it allows you to view things from a perspective of openness, willingness, and adaptiveness. The theory of detachment is especially helpful to your adaptability, as detachment allows you to release the need to cling to any specific state of being or experience. This way, as life naturally changes, you are able to accept and embrace all aspects of change. The more you allow yourself to embrace this perspective, the stronger your adaptability skills will become.

CHAPTER 19
Exercise The Power Of Creativity

Creativity carries a phenomenal impact on your capacity to embrace life force energy and expand your mind power. Everything in existence got there because of creativity, and the power of creativity has driven us to exponential heights. From creating technology to discovering language and expanding our self-awareness, creativity has enabled us to reach impressive heights as a society, and as a species.

Kundalini energy, and life force energy, both carry with them significant energies of creation. Moving that energy through you and into the world surrounding you is a phenomenal way to work with that energy and create more space for it in your life. As you continue to call on it and use it, it will continue to flow through you naturally and with more significant strength.

Through creation, you gain many values. Manifestation, invention, and experience are all empowered through the energy of creation. Moreover, you experience a deep connection to the present moment and an exhilarating state of flow that drastically impacts your overall sense of wellbeing.

Creativity Is at the Root of Manifesting

Manifesting is a skill everyone desires to improve in their lives, and it is one we all have the capacity to embody. As you awaken your kundalini and expand your mind power, you gain the capacity to tap into your infinite creative abilities and manifest anything you desire. People have been manifesting since the beginning of time, conjuring up images in their minds of the things and lives they desired and calling them in through phenomenal manifesting abilities. At the root of it all was the life force energy and their capacity to create.

To expand into your manifesting abilities, you must first call on the power of your imagination. You may find it easy to imagine all that you desire, or you may find you have to be patient and practice working within your imagination to expand your abilities. If you struggle with using your imagination, meditation is a great opportunity to expand your creative abilities and draw forth images of all you desire to your mind. It also helps to clear away any limiting beliefs by pretending that there are no caps and limitations to what you can attract into your life. This often feels entirely unnatural and even directly opposing everything you have learned in your life; however, manifesting and embracing the power of your imagination are your birthright. Everyone has the power to manifest, as we are all born with this natural power.

If you find you struggle with manifesting or expanding your mind power through creativity, it often helps to scale down what you seek to create. Rather than attempting to call in an entire lifestyle and massive goals from the start, consider looking at opportunities to manifest smaller things. Manifest the ability to visualize your desires in your mind or to call smaller things into your life, such as a certain symbol or experience you desire to have. Once you become fluent in calling forward these smaller experiences, manifesting larger desires becomes easier, because you become used to following your intuition and life force energies.

Unlocking the Power of Your Creativity

To fully unlock the power of creativity through kundalini, you must first tap into your kundalini energies. The farther you dive into your awakening and the activation of your life force energy, creativity naturally starts to emerge. Often, practitioners who dig deep into their journey find they suddenly have a desire to sing, paint, write, or engage in another creative outlet. At the root of each of our minds is a deep desire to create something, as a form of expression and an opportunity to explore the world and universe through alternate senses. Art has always been fundamental to our society, and our individual wellbeing, so it makes sense that we thrive when we call it into our lives.

If you desire to call on and engage the power of your creativity in a specific moment, it can be helpful to first engage in a kundalini yoga session. This way, you embody kundalini within your body, activate your life force energy, and open space for you to be influenced by the world around you. Throughout your session, you may find inspiration for something to create, or the momentum to work toward a creation you had already been inspired to take action on. Or, you might find that you need to rest in meditation following a session for several moments to call in the inspiration to create. Regardless, you will inevitably feel the energy of creation move through you, so long as you remain open and willing to receive it.

Understand that, upon activating your creative energies, you may not be good at whichever outlet you choose to engage in. At first, you will be a beginner like anyone else. However, you will rapidly uncover the independent essence of your creativity that makes your work unique to you. Further, you will discover that the urge you have to create provides you with a sense of momentum that keeps you working toward developing your greatness each day. This is how people become excellent at what they do.

Steps to Expand Your Creativity

Invoking life force energy to stimulate your creativity is an excellent way to tap into this power; however, there are other practical steps you can take toward developing your creativity expanding mind power, too. By taking practical action, you create space for the spiritual energy of creativity to root in and expand through you, effectively expanding your life force energy and your mind power.

One excellent way to expand your creativity is through collaboration. Being curious and collaborating with others enables you to open yourself up to learning from them, while also being inspired by the presence of their energy and the unique energy they manifest themselves, too. Together, you might discover that your collaboration itself presents a form of energy that triggers inspiration and motivates each of you to embrace and live in the energy of creativity.

Following your passion, or those loving urges you feel inside yourself is another excellent way to expand your creativity. When you do something you love, you have a deep hunger within you to continue pursuing that activity and learning more about it, which stimulates your momentum and the development of your creative energy.

If following others' or expanding into existing momentum does not do the trick, you can always focus on retreating, instead. Sometimes, unplugging, giving yourself time away, and taking a genuine break is plenty to inspire you with new creative energies. Rather than trying to force your existing routine, or the creation of anything, fully surrender to a break. Go for peaceful walks, take care of yourself, enjoy plenty of relaxation, and make time for calmness, and see if inspiration strikes during those peaceful moments. Often, it is within the stillness and silence of life that our greatest inspiration strikes, as we finally pause and relax long enough to give it the space it needs to manifest.

If that doesn't work, you can always stimulate your creativity through idea lists and the practice of choosing the worst idea possible. Start by taking your idea notebook and writing down every idea you have, no matter how significant or insignificant it is. Do not confine yourself around what you ought to create, either. Write down everything from inventions and story ideas to paintings and artwork you can create, and keep going until you genuinely run out of ideas. Then, pick the worst idea from your book and begin taking action on that idea. Often, following the worst idea and genuinely putting the plan in action can motivate you to uncover a great idea, which will inspire you to design something new and impressive.

Integrating Creativity Into Your Everyday Life

Compartmentalizing your life is a sure way to confuse yourself and lose out on the value of a life that is orchestrated to be an overall experience. Far too often, people want to segregate the different areas of their lives as an opportunity to force each of these categories into a small, neat box. Unfortunately, you cannot expand in one area of your life without expanding in all, and if you shrink in one area of life, you will experience shrinkage in all areas, too. Separating everything into categories prevents you from harmonizing your experience and expression and embracing the many values life has to offer.

Rather than segregating your life into different categories, learn to view your entire life as a canvas, and integrate creativity into everything you do. Discover how you can creatively apply lessons from one area of your life to all areas of your life, stay hungry enough to expand in every way possible, and put effort into creating a life that fulfills you overall. Through this, your entire life becomes a canvas that you get to use to create the life you desire.

Do everything with intention and creativity, looking for ways to bring self-expression and meaning into each step. Whether it be turning your nightly hygiene routine into a meaningful ritual, or the way you eat into a form of self-expression, discover how to overturn mundane tasks with creativity. Integrating creativity into all areas of your life enables you to engage in the energy of life and reap as much joy from it as you possibly can.

If you desire to embrace the energy of creativity for the power of manifestation, this is an excellent opportunity to reach that stage, too. With each task you engage in, creatively integrate elements of your desires into it. Visualize yourself pursuing your dreams, see yourself experiencing it from an expanded state of awareness, and behave as though you have already created the experiences of your dreams. Through this, you expand your creativity through imagination and playing pretend, while also using energy to create the life you desire in every way possible. This is how you gain the opportunity to become the most creative person possible, while enjoying the energy of authentic self-expression.

CONCLUSION

Congratulations on reading *Kundalini*! This book was intended to show you the many ways you can integrate kundalini into your everyday life so you can live from an expanded point of consciousness and perception. Awakening kundalini energy is about far more than just following the mainstream trends or a journey your friend invited you on that you unknowingly agreed to. Kundalini is a personal journey that is intended to support you with accessing the entirety of your energy so you can activate it and use it in your everyday life. Life is significantly more meaningful and enjoyable when you embrace it with your maximum energy, and continue to expand into your energy so you can experience more out of life.

I hope reading this book has encouraged you to discover just how impactful a kundalini awakening is, and how extensively this energy can transform your life. Beyond connecting you to abundant life force energy, it can also provide you with the capacity to approach life from an entirely unique perspective. Engaging in life from this grounded, empowering angle enables you to gain everything that life has to offer, while also balancing your energies so you can experience greater enlightenment.

Enlightenment and the process of awakening is, genuinely, a never ending journey. So long as you are alive on earth, you have the potential to continually expand your energy and mind power. If you desire full enlightenment and the experience of the heavens and gods, it is worth it to continue to explore how this energy can be integrated into your life. Not only will this expand your enlightenment, but it also deepens the joy and fulfillment you gain from life itself.

After reading this book, it is worth it to continue studying the nature of kundalini and the many ways you can integrate this energy into your life. Investing in study is a wonderful way to expand your perspective, gain insight into how you can integrate life force energy into your earthly experience, and increase the value you gain from life itself. It also allows you to carefully remove yourself from the earthly experiences of suffering, providing you with the opportunity to heal and experience greater success in your life.

If you have not already, I encourage you to integrate a daily kundalini routine into your life, which enables you to tap into your life force energy and experience the depths of it. As you continue to tap in, your understanding of kundalini and life force energy will expand, offering you greater insight into the energy of life and the purpose of your life.

Before you go, I ask that you please take a moment to review *Kundalini* on Amazon. Your honest feedback would be greatly appreciated, as it provides others' with the opportunity to uncover the value to be gained from this book.

Thank you, and best of luck with your awakening and the expansion of your mind power!

www.ingramcontent.com/pod-product-compliance
Lightning Source LLC
Chambersburg PA
CBHW081345070526
44578CB00005B/732